KU-754-978

Contents

A PLACE IN HISTORY   2

ROYAL GREENWICH   4

THE QUEEN'S HOUSE   6

THE OLD ROYAL NAVAL COLLEGE   10

THE ROYAL OBSERVATORY   16

CUTTY SARK   22

THE NATIONAL MARITIME MUSEUM   26

THE THAMES AND THE TOWN   32

THE PARK AND ITS BORDERS   34

A GREENWICH CHRONOLOGY   38

GAZETTEER   40

INFORMATION FOR VISITORS   48

HOW TO USE THE GUIDE
The first part outlines the story of historic Greenwich.
To help you find your way around, the Gazetteer gives brief
information about buildings and attractions, whose positions
are numbered on the map in the back cover. The map
also includes locations covered in the Information for
Visitors section.

A Place in History

On Thames's bank in silent thought we stood,
Where Greenwich smiles upon the silver flood:
Struck with the seat that gave Eliza birth,
We kneel, and kiss the consecrated earth.

Samuel Johnson (lived in Greenwich, 1737)

When Dr Johnson celebrated Greenwich as a favourite scene in 1738, nearly twenty years before Canaletto's great painting, it was a riverside village on the fringe of London. This already had a long history: towards the east side of the Park a mound denotes the site of a small Roman shrine of the first century AD, and to the west a cluster of mounds indicates an Anglo-Saxon burial ground. Strategically placed next to the main land and water routes from continental Europe to the capital, Greenwich was one of the main bases for the Danish conquest of England in the early eleventh century.

In Johnson's time, the main activities at Greenwich were centred on the Royal Naval Hospital, founded in 1694 and replacing the now-vanished royal palace where King Henry VIII and Queen Elizabeth I were born. Here Anne of Denmark, consort of King James I, had commissioned Inigo Jones to build the Queen's House, which, completed by Henrietta Maria, wife of King Charles I, now forms the centrepiece of the National Maritime Museum. Until 1869 the Hospital was home to the blue-coated and battle-scarred Pensioners of the Royal Navy, before serving as the Royal Naval College and, from 1983, as the Joint Services Defence College for the advanced training of officers.

These buildings beside the River Thames, with the first of all royal parks as a backdrop, form the finest classical architectural landscape in Britain, crowned on top of the hill by King Charles II's Royal Observatory. Here the Astronomer Royal, John Flamsteed, was instructed by the King to map the stars so that the sailors on whom British maritime pre-eminence depended could fix their position at sea. Since 1884, the world has set its clocks relative to the time of day on the meridian of Greenwich, Longitude 0°, the baseline of the International Time Zone system.

No other site in Britain contains so many outstanding buildings by our foremost classical architects. The town, which was transformed from a medieval fishing village into an elegant Georgian domestic and commercial centre, bears the imprint of over 300 years of growth and adaptation. Fine private houses frame the Park, and the town's nineteenth-century market and shopping parades bear witness to a flourishing commercial and maritime community. Until the spread of river pollution in the late nineteenth century, whitebait came up-river as far as Greenwich and were a local delicacy, attracting celebrities and others alike to such inns as the surviving Trafalgar Tavern, and The Ship, which once stood where the most beautiful of sailing ships, *Cutty Sark*, now rests in dry-dock.

The kings and queens, the Pensioners, Samuel Pepys, Dr Johnson, Nelson, Dickens and others, distinguished and unknown, have gone; but if they were to return, they would still easily recognize the Park, with boundaries largely unchanged since 1433, the great buildings and the busy urban scene. Only the river itself is less populated but, even here, the whitebait are coming back. Historic Greenwich has largely survived, an island in the city, where the story of Britain and the sea, and of time itself, can be enjoyed in a unique architectural and landscape setting.

TIME FROM GREENWICH
'H4', John Harrison's prize-winning chronometer of 1759, which finally solved the problem of fixing longitude at sea.

GREENWICH HOSPITAL
Painted by Canaletto at about the time of its completion in 1751, with the Queen's House, Park and distant Observatory.

Royal Greenwich

GREENWICH HAS MAINTAINED royal connections for 600 years. During the sixteenth century, the palace at Greenwich was one of the principal Crown residences. During Henry VIII's reign, from 1509 to 1547, it was the scene of constant diplomatic activity as the first, or last, port of call for visiting ambassadors from mainland Europe. Following the building of Whitehall Palace in the 1530s, Greenwich became a royal country retreat and a particular favourite of the Stuart queens Anne of Denmark and Henrietta Maria. Later royal patronage brought the building of the Royal Observatory and the Royal Hospital for Seamen. More recently the royal connection has been maintained through the Royal Naval College and the National Maritime Museum, of which HRH The Duke of Edinburgh is Patron and HRH The Duke of York a Trustee.

Greenwich was a royal manor from at least the fourteenth century, and a new Thames-side house was built here by Humphrey, Duke of Gloucester, regent from 1426 to his nephew, the young king Henry VI. In 1433 he enclosed 200 acres of heathland, woodland and pasture with a wooden fence to form the Park, and on the site where the Royal Observatory now stands built the small castle known as Duke Humphrey's Tower. This was later remodelled and used by Henry VIII as lodgings for one of his mistresses. After Humphrey's death in 1447, the riverside house, known as Bellacourt, became the residence of Margaret of Anjou, wife of Henry VI. Renamed Placentia, the manor house was rebuilt as a palace by Henry VII, who added a new front towards the Thames.

Henry VIII, a compulsive builder and an enthusiastic horseman and jouster, made further alterations. He rebuilt the chapel, built stables and added a tiltyard with towers and a viewing gallery. Martial displays, in which the King played a vigorous part, became highlights of ambassadorial visits, the signing of treaties being followed by celebratory jousts, banqueting, the performance of masques and dancing until dawn. Here also he established his armoury and, nearby, his two great naval dockyards – at Woolwich to the east and Deptford to the west.

'FAYRE GREENWICH CASTLE'
Duke Humphrey's Tower as remodelled by Henry VIII and James I, overlooking Greenwich Palace. By Wenceslaus Hollar, 1637.

GEORGE CLIFFORD, EARL OF CUMBERLAND
In Nicholas Hilliard's miniature, he is shown as Queen Elizabeth's champion in the 'Star' suit of Greenwich armour.

HENRY VIII
A portrait after Holbein. Both Henry and Elizabeth I (top) were born at Greenwich and used it as a main residence.

His daughter Elizabeth maintained the banqueting houses and added a new one in 1559. But, although she spent most summers at Greenwich, she did little building here. The courtier Lord Northampton revamped Duke Humphrey's Tower as the ornamental castle of Millefleur, a pleasure house

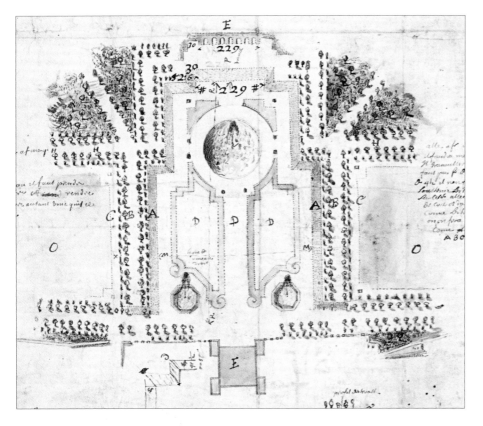

THE PARK REDESIGNED
The central parterre and raised side avenues on this 1660s plan by André le Nôtre are all that exists of this uncompleted scheme. The Queen's House, showing proposed corner pavilions, is at the bottom.

one of these ranges, now known as the King Charles Court, was begun, in 1664. It was left incomplete and boarded-up as work petered out around 1669. It was this building, then alarmingly in use as a gunpowder store, that Queen Mary in 1694 granted for conversion into a hospital for seamen.

Charles's intentions for the Park were comparably ambitious. A surviving plan was prepared by the great French garden designer André le Nôtre, creator of the parks at Versailles and Vaux-le-Vicomte, though it was only partly executed. Implementation of the scheme was the responsibility of Sir William Boreman, among others. He planted many of the tree avenues and in 1661–2 cut the Giant Steps that linked the upper and lower parts of the Park. Four of these are still visible on the eroded slope up to the Observatory. At the south end of the Park, the major and minor avenues radiated from a semicircle of trees flanked by contrived wildernesses, one of which, the Great Wilderness, survives as a small area of wood and pasture for a tiny herd of deer.

overlooking the Thames, for use as a retreat, complete with kitchen, wine cellar and private garden. At the same time King James I replaced the fence around the Park with a brick wall approximately two miles (3.2 km) in length and 12 feet (3.5 m) high, at a cost of about £2,000. In the palace, he added a stone-vaulted undercroft beneath the timber hall and built new lodgings for his wife, Anne of Denmark. Shortly afterwards he assigned the palace to her, and she began improvements to the gardens that culminated in her employment of Inigo Jones to design the Queen's House.

While the palace offered little exceptional architecture to admire, Anne's Italianate garden was a source of delight. Devised by the French garden designer and hydraulic engineer, Salomon de Caus, with fountains, statues pouring water, an aviary and a grotto encrusted in mother-of-pearl, mussels and all sorts of shells, this appeared so artfully natural that in the view of a French visitor, 'it seems that art had hardly any part'. Anne's concentration on the garden and the building of her adjacent retreat, the Queen's House, was continued by Henrietta Maria.

It was not until the Restoration of King Charles II in 1660 that royal attention was shifted back onto the palace itself. Charles determined to replace it with a modern classical structure of three ranges open to the river, designed by John Webb, the pupil of Inigo Jones. Stuart finances were perennially uncertain, however, and only

GREENWICH, ABOUT 1680
Vorsterman's painting shows the Queen's House, the incomplete wing of Charles II's new palace, the Observatory and the ruins of the Tudor Palace.

The Queen's House

THIS ITALIANATE HOUSE OF delight, designed by Inigo Jones, is one of the most important buildings in British architectural history, emblematic of the pure classicism that Jones introduced in the service of the Stuart court. Work was begun in 1616 for Queen Anne of Denmark but had stopped by the time of her death in 1619, when it was only one storey high. Queen Henrietta Maria ordered work to restart on the house in 1629. She was still engaged on the lavish fitting-out of the interior when the Civil War broke out in 1642, destroying the Stuart idyll, sending the King to his death and the Queen into exile until 1662.

The Queen's House was one of the first truly classical buildings in England. Having visited Italy and studied extensively its buildings and gardens, Inigo Jones here created a small-scale version of a Renaissance villa as a private retreat for the Stuart queens. His specific model was the Medici villa of Poggio a Caiano, outside Florence, by Giuliano da Sangallo. Instead of Sangallo's central salon, however, Jones designed the House as a bridge over the Deptford to Woolwich road that divided the palace gardens from the Park, replacing the Tudor gatehouse that had hitherto performed this function.

Originally the House was, in effect, two separate buildings, linked by a single central room over the road at first-floor level, and it was rightly regarded at the time as a 'curious device'. The addition of two further bridge rooms in the 1660s has to some extent obscured the original plan-form, turning Jones's H into a square. The road itself was moved north to its present position in about 1699.

The House has had a chequered history, remaining in the ownership of

THE HOUSE FROM THE NORTH
The first purely classical Renaissance building in England. Jones may have intended this façade to have painted decoration, as a permanent backdrop for welcoming important visitors on the terrace. Eighteenth-century sashes now replace the original leaded mullion-and-transom windows.

INIGO JONES
Little is known of Jones before he gained fame as a designer of court masques. The Queen's House, begun for Anne of Denmark and completed for Henrietta Maria, is his most influential building. This is Hogarth's version of a portrait by Van Dyck.

the Crown, but at various periods being occupied by the Ranger of Greenwich Park, then by the Governor of the Royal Hospital and later by Greenwich Hospital School, eventually becoming the centre-piece of the National Maritime Museum. King George I was received here in 1714, following his first landing in England, an event depicted in the Painted Hall of the Royal Hospital. In 1736 the marriage of Frederick, Prince of Wales, to Augusta, Princess of Saxe-Gotha, the great-grandmother of Queen Victoria, was celebrated in the House.

The cubic, galleried, two-storey hall, the dramatic Tulip Stairs and the plaster-work of the mid-seventeenth-century bridge rooms, as well as the view of the Park from the loggia, give a flavour of the grandeur intended by the royal occupants. However, much of the decorative painting commissioned by Henrietta Maria remained incomplete, and many high-quality paintings that had been installed were dispersed by the Parliamentarian government after the execution of Charles I. Within the hall and the state rooms on the north side of the house were paintings of cautionary delight and instruction: Orazio Gentileschi's 'Finding of Moses', 'Joseph and Potiphar's Wife', 'Lot and his Daughters' and 'Apollo and the Muses'; his daughter Artemisia's 'Tarquin and Lucretia'; and on the ceiling of the hall, his 'Allegory of Peace and Arts under the English Crown'. The original ceiling was

Queen Anne of Denmark (1574–1619)

The queen of King James I, and sister of Christian IV of Denmark, Anne took up residence in London in 1604. She was a great patron of the arts, particularly architecture and gardening, which she indulged to great effect at Greenwich after being granted the manor and palace in 1613. Her close association with Inigo Jones extended beyond his design of the Queen's House. She also participated in those quintessentially Stuart entertain-ments, the court masques, for which Jones made hundreds of designs, most notably in collaboration with Ben Jonson, between 1605 and 1640. Through Queen Anne's influence, the masque became a polished, sophisticated and very expensive art form, combining music, verse, costume and dance, with sets and staging notable for their ingenuity and spectacular effects. Anne's delight in spectacle, which contributed to her dying heavily in debt, extended to her own appearance: she had a passion for clothes and jewellery, of which she built up a significant collection. A dedicated leader of fashion, at least one of her portraits was amended to reflect a more up-to-date hairstyle.

ANNE OF DENMARK *A portrait by the early Stuart court painter John de Critz, about 1603–5.*

removed to Marlborough House in the early eighteenth century; a computer-generated copy was shown in its place from 1990 to 1999. The Queen's Bedchamber has the original ceiling coving painted in 'grotesque-work', probably by Matthew Gooderick, who worked also at Somerset House. The central panel shows Aurora, goddess of the dawn, dispersing the shades of night, by an unknown artist.

FROM THE PARK *The House was a bridge from the old palace gardens to the Park over the Deptford to Woolwich road, until this was moved in about 1699. The 1807 colonnades are on the same line as the high brick walls that originally flanked the road, where, reputedly, Sir Walter Raleigh laid down his cloak for Elizabeth I to cross dryshod.*

Queen Henrietta Maria (1609–69)

Henrietta Maria, the youngest daughter of Henri IV of France and Marie de' Medici, married King Charles I in 1625. They were for some years on poor terms, partly because of his fondness for the Duke of Buckingham, whom she disliked, and partly because of her reliance on a Catholic household, which he distrusted. However, the assassination of the Duke and her loving reconciliation with the King in 1629 made the 1630s some of the happiest years of her life. The Queen was a woman of gaiety, humour, charm and vivacity who loved masques, plays and games and brought a lightness and naturalness to the court. She was a perfect foil to her sober and correct husband. The Queen's House, completed for her by Inigo Jones, was essentially a private summer retreat for the royal couple. At the outbreak of Civil War in 1642, the Queen fled to the Continent, not returning to England until 1662, when she briefly reoccupied the House before establishing herself at Somerset House. In 1665 she returned to France, where she died.

ROYAL PAIR
Henrietta Maria, in a Van Dyck studio version of a portrait he painted at Greenwich; with her husband, Charles I, after Van Dyck.

The Queen's House, through style, position and status, determined the direction of all later developments on the palace site, including the principal axis through the Park. Small but perfect, it has had an impact far in excess of its scale through the purity of its fully achieved classicism and the sentimental feelings prompted by the tragic circumstances that ended its brief royal occupation. When Charles II discussed with the diarist John Evelyn his 'intentions of building his Palace of Greenwich and quite demolishing the old', he seems to have had in mind an aggrandisement of the Queen's House, with corner pavilions, rather than starting entirely afresh. Foundations for pavilions were indeed dug, but the plan was superseded by John Webb's design for a three-range palace. This would have cut across the vista from the Queen's House to the river, which (though not there when it was built) became sacrosanct when excluded by Queen Mary II from her grant of land for the Naval Hospital in 1694. She reserved to the Crown a strip of land the width of the house in order to provide a route to and from the Thames. The first beneficiary of this view following the demolition of the old palace was the Hospital Governor Sir William Gifford, who in 1712 ordered two oak seats for the terrace, the better to enjoy it.

ART IN THE QUEEN'S HOUSE
The house is now used to display aspects of the National Maritime Museum's superb art collection. This view shows paintings in the East Bridge Room.

THE TULIP STAIRS
The first centrally unsupported spiral stair in Britain. Planned from the beginning of the House, it was completed in about 1635 at the height of the European 'tulip craze'. Its name derives from the pattern of the wrought-iron balustrade, and it originally led from the ground floor to a polygonal turret on the roof.

The Old Royal Naval College

THE CONSTRUCTION OF this magnificent group of riverside buildings was begun in 1696 to the designs of Sir Christopher Wren and Nicholas Hawksmoor. Originally the Royal Hospital for Seamen, it was a remarkably grand almshouse for former Royal Navy seamen who for reasons of age or disability were unable to maintain themselves. Occupation by these 'Greenwich Pensioners' continued until 1869, when the buildings were adapted for use as the Royal Naval College, from 1873. The finest piece of monumental classical architecture in England, the College has within its walls two acclaimed masterpieces of interior decoration – Sir James Thornhill's Baroque Painted Hall and the Neoclassical Chapel by James Stuart and William Newton.

Queen Mary II determined that 'the house at Greenwich' (the single range of the projected palace of Charles II) should be 'converted and employed as a hospital for seamen', and that the adjoining area, still occupied by the decayed Tudor palace, should be allocated for its expansion. The increase in the importance of the Navy over the previous 150 years had not been matched by any appropriate provision for those wounded or worn out in its service. The Royal Hospital at Chelsea had been founded in 1682 for pensioners of the Army, following the earlier example of Louis XV's Hôtel des Invalides, dating from 1670. It was to provide for similarly wounded or invalid seamen that Queen Mary, after the severe casualties sustained at the victorious naval engagement at La Hogue in 1692, sought to establish equivalent accommodation for the Navy.

Mary died in a smallpox epidemic in 1694, and the impetus for building the Hospital was taken up by her grieving, 'mightily afflicted' husband, King William III. By July 1695, £8,000 had been raised,

GREENWICH FROM THE RIVER
The 'Canaletto' view of the Royal Naval College and the Queen's House.

GREENWICH PENSIONERS ON TRAFALGAR DAY, 1835
Those shown include Nelson's servant Tom Allen (holding his portrait, left), men from the crew of Victory at Trafalgar and boys from the Greenwich Hospital School. The picture is by S. P. Denning after John Burnet's painting of 1837, which was bought by the Duke of Wellington.

PENSIONERS DINING

When Thornhill began decorating the Painted Hall in 1708, dining for the Hospital Pensioners was moved to the undercrofts below the Hall and the Chapel, remaining there until the Hospital closed.

and William himself promised an endowment of £2,000 a year. In charitable spirit, Christopher Wren, formally appointed Surveyor in 1696, worked free of charge. He was assisted by Nicholas Hawksmoor, who became Clerk of Works in 1698, a post he held through various vicissitudes until 1735, and by John James, assistant to Hawksmoor from 1705, and later joint Clerk with him. Although Sir John Vanbrugh was a member of the Board of Directors from 1703, and Surveyor in succession to Wren from 1716, he had little part in the design. The main lines of the Hospital, including all the foundations, were laid out by Wren, with the 'courts' themselves being designed by himself and Hawksmoor. The exception is the last to be erected, the Queen Mary Court, built by Thomas Ripley.

Despite the promising start, the project was bedevilled by constant financial uncertainty. The construction was spread over four main phases between 1696 and 1751, with works to complete and regularize the site continuing into the nineteenth century. Within three years of

starting, the scheme was £9,000 in debt, growing to £19,000 by 1702. It was not until 1735 with the granting of the rents and profits of the Earl of Derwentwater's estate, following his execution in 1716 for supporting the early Jacobite rising, that the Hospital finances were put on a secure footing. It is in fact remarkable that the Hospital was completed at all, and still more astonishing that it was built so magnificently, particularly since the perpetual refrain of the Directors was for more and more economies. Even

Hawksmoor, often criticized for excess, played his part in looking for bargains, in 1714 snapping up a block of marble suitable for a statue of King William for £125. This came to nothing until Rysbrack used it it to carve his statue of George II in Imperial Roman guise, set up in the Grand Square of the Hospital in 1735 at the expense of the Governor, Sir John Jennings.

Hawksmoor was later to refer to Queen Mary's 'fixt Intention for Magnificence' when founding the Hospital. Not only was it designed to fulfil the duty felt by the monarch towards men disabled through serving their country, but to do so in a manner that conspicuously demonstrated the political and naval power of the state. The building of the Hospital, on the river leading to the capital, was a political as well as a philanthropic act. Queen

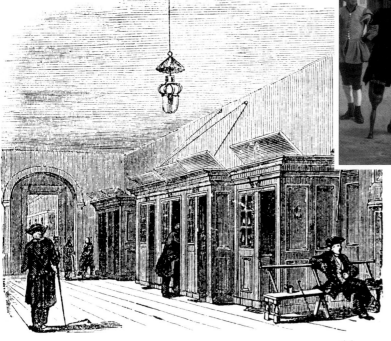

THE PENSIONER'S STORY

Visitors to Greenwich listen to a Pensioner's yarn; by Thomas Davidson.

LIFE ON THE WARDS

The Hospital buildings largely comprised huge wards, with panelled cabins for individual men or small groups.

Mary's 'Intention' was heeded by all of the architects involved in the prolonged building campaign, a fact borne out by the final cost of about £400,000 for carrying out Wren's design.

The four blocks of the Hospital – the King Charles, Queen Anne, King William and Queen Mary Courts – take their architectural cue from John Webb's original palace proposal. The coupled columns, which bind the design together, appear first on the river-front of his King Charles building, are reflected in the identical Queen Anne building opposite, then reappear at ground level in the colonnades of the King William and Queen Mary buildings, and at the upper level in the drums of the magnificent domes, which frame the view to the Queen's House and the Park.

The Queen's House was far too small to provide the dominating central feature that might have been expected in a classical architectural complex of this size and ambition. In his design for a cross-wing for a palace, Webb had proposed a central dome. Wren repeated this, in vain, in his first scheme for the Hospital, then had to think again, towards a less obvious solution. As a result, responding to the constraint imposed by Inigo Jones's master-piece, Wren produced a masterpiece of his own, with two domes rather than one and an open centre that enabled him to achieve a remarkable complementary synthesis between architecture and landscape.

The accommodation was a mixture of small rooms, with space for between four and eight curtained beds, and larger 'wards' containing wainscotted or curtained 'cabins'. In the Queen Anne building one of these large wards, the Collingwood Room, survives on the ground floor.

THE QUEEN MARY COURT
This, the second domed court, was the last to be completed, in 1751. The dome was nearly destroyed when Ripley's original Chapel below accidentally burnt out in January 1779.

THE BOWLING ALLEY
Situated under the colonnade of the Queen Mary Court, this is believed to have been installed in the 1860s, towards the end of the building's life as a hospital.

'THE IMMORTALITY OF NELSON'
Designed by Sir Benjamin West, this version of his own painting shows Neptune offering up Nelson's body to Britannia. It was modelled in Mrs Coade's artificial stone for the tympanum of the King William courtyard in 1812.

The Painted Hall

The painter James Thornhill was rewarded with £6,685 – and a knighthood – for this, the major work of his career; he was paid £3 per square yard for the ceiling and £1 for the walls. The finest piece of allegorical Baroque decorative painting by an English artist, it was carried out in two stages, the main Hall in 1708–12 and the upper Hall in 1718–25. It immediately became a tourist attraction, with a small charge for entry. The enormous oval centre design of the main ceiling proclaims the virtues of constitutional monarchy. The founders of the Hospital, King William and Queen Mary, sit enthroned among the Virtues, with Concord and Peace in attendance. William hands the cap of Liberty to Europe as Louis XIV of France, representing Arbitrary Power, crouches beneath his feet. Elsewhere, Time exposes Truth, and Wisdom and Strength destroy the Vices. Naval power is celebrated at each end of the ceiling – a British man-of-war laden with trophies at the upper end, and a captured Spanish ship at the lower.

The dependence of naval and mercantile power on navigation and the mapping of the stars is marked by the inclusion of many scientific references and the presence of the astronomers Tycho Brahe, Copernicus and John Flamsteed, the first Astronomer Royal.

In the upper Hall, in rather more domestic manner, Thornhill

commemorates the Protestant succession. On the ceiling here are Queen Mary's sister Queen Anne and her husband, Prince George of Denmark, who was Lord High Admiral. The left-hand wall shows the landing of William III, as Prince of Orange, at Torbay in 1688. On the right is the landing of King George I at Greenwich in 1714. On the end wall – the 'great front' – he and his family preside over Naval Victory, Peace and Plenty, while on the lower right side Thornhill himself gestures towards his composition. On either side of the arch on the return to the main Hall, the design reminds the visitor of the maritime basis for all this splendour: Plenty pours riches into the lap of Commerce while Britannia with her trident ensures Public Security.

THE CEILING
Measuring 108 x 50 feet (33 x 15.5 m), and about 50 feet (15.5 m) above the floor, this took Thornhill five years to paint.

The Pensioners began to arrive in 1704, numbering 350 by 1709 but not reaching 1,000 until 1738. The capacity of the buildings was increased later, particularly in the Queen Mary building, erected between 1735 and 1751, where the Surveyor, Thomas Ripley, departed from the Wren/Hawksmoor script and produced a more economical and far less dramatic design than the King William building opposite. By squeezing people together and reducing the width of dining

tables, except those used by officers, and by building a dedicated infirmary in the 1760s, more and more Pensioners could be accommodated. Some small steps were taken to make communal life more bearable – from 1741 the men were allowed two shirts a week in the summer rather than just one. Their number reached 2,000 in 1770 and a maximum of 2,710 in 1814.

With such numbers, two sittings for meals were necessary, in the two

magnificent colonnaded dining rooms beneath the Painted Hall and the Chapel, each served by its own kitchen. The Painted Hall was used for dining only on exceptional occasions. The diet was plain, and repetitive: mutton on two days, beef on three, with pea soup and cheese on the other two. Two quarts of beer a day were provided, piped to the dining areas from the Hospital's own brewhouse. Smoking was not encouraged because of the risk of fire, but since sailors were regarded as

The Chapel

The original Chapel was destroyed by fire in 1779 following New Year celebrations in the tailor's shop, 'wherein the men . . . had mingled holiday rejoicing too much with their labours'. The rebuilt Chapel, by James 'Athenian' Stuart and William Newton, is a Neoclassical masterpiece richly decorated with a combination of plasterwork, done by hand, and cast-work from Eleanor Coade's artificial stone factory. The painter Benjamin West designed the four Coade stone statues of Faith, Hope, Charity and Meekness, which are placed in the entrance vestibule, but his major contribution to the Chapel was the altarpiece: 'The Preservation of St Paul after Shipwreck in the Island of Malta'. Intended to appeal to a congregation of sailors, now secure from previous perils, it shows Paul miraculously unhurt by the bite of a viper concealed

in the wood for the fire lit to dry out the survivors, and casting the snake back in the flames.

The Chapel – which has excellent acoustics – also contains a superb organ of 1787 by Samuel Green set above the entrance door, itself with a finely carved marble surround by John Bacon RA. This is flanked by monuments to Admirals Keats and Hardy, successive Governors of the Hospital in the 1830s. Hardy was captain of *Victory* at Trafalgar and is buried in the Hospital Mausoleum, just over the road. There is also a large monument to Sir John Franklin's lost Arctic expedition of 1845 behind the altar.

THE CHAPEL
The marble floor is laid to a nautical cable pattern, and the pulpit is the top section of the original 'three-decker' which used to stand centrally in front of West's altarpiece.

THE 'BASE BLOCK'
The western range of the King Charles Court was Wren's first addition to the eastern part built in the 1660s. It was remodelled in its present form by John Yenn in 1812–15.

being 'very great smokers', provision was made, first in the room next to the Painted Hall, subsequently known as the Nelson Room, then in the Chalk Walk, a long and draughty basement beneath the east colonnade, which later was to house a skittles alley. It was freely acknowledged in the last years of the Hospital that life for the Pensioners was extremely dull. In the view of the First Lord of the Admiralty, the Duke of Somerset, most passed their days 'in a state of listless idleness and mental vacuity, until recalled at fixed intervals to their meals or their beds. It is not surprising that old sailors so circumstanced should resort to the alehouse or worse places'.

In 1860, a Commission appointed to look into the management and economy of the Hospital found that the cost of running it was disproportionate to the number of Pensioners. In 1869, in the

MASKS IN STONE
Carved by Robert Jones for the King William range in the early eighteenth century but never used. At present they are kept in the 1606 undercroft that James I inserted beneath the Tudor banqueting house, which survives under the Queen Anne Court.

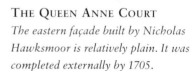

words of *The Times*, 'the walls of Greenwich Hospital were closed'. In 1873 the Admiralty transferred its Naval College, established at Portsmouth in 1841, to form the Royal Naval College at Greenwich, 'for the education of officers of all ranks above midshipman in all branches of theoretical and scientific study bearing on their profession'. After a century of occupation of the buildings, the 'University of the Navy' was expanded in 1983 to become the Joint Services Defence College.

Following the Government's decision in 1995 to move service training facilities elsewhere, responsibility for the College was passed in 1998 to the Greenwich Foundation, a charitable management trust specially formed to ensure that the buildings and their surroundings are cared for and used appropriately, and that public access is maintained. The principal buildings are now occupied by the University of Greenwich, with the exception of the King Charles Court, next to the river, which became home to Trinity College of Music in 2001. The Foundation has direct responsibility for the Painted Hall, the Chapel and the grounds.

THE QUEEN ANNE COURT
The eastern façade built by Nicholas Hawksmoor is relatively plain. It was completed externally by 1705.

THE KING WILLIAM COURTYARD
Pensioners in the courtyard as seen by James Holland, about 1850. Hawksmoor's striking inner façade of the western range (left) was completed around 1708. The stone-wreathed circular windows and swags on the pilaster heads include seashells and other marine elements. The cobbled courtyard undulates strongly in a pattern designed to help drainage.

15

The Royal Observatory

THE MODEST APPEARANCE OF the group of buildings that stands on the hill in Greenwich Park belies its significance, for it is here that international time begins. Since 1884, the world has set its clocks according to the time of day on the meridian of Greenwich, Longitude 0°, which is defined by the Airy Transit Circle, installed in 1850–1. This was a development from the original purpose of the Observatory, which was set out when Charles II appointed John Flamsteed as his first Astronomer Royal in 1675, instructing him, 'to apply himself with the most exact care and diligence to the rectifying the tables of the motions of the heavens, and the places of the fixed stars, so as to find out the so much-desired longitude of places for the perfecting the art of navigation'.

A strong presence at sea was crucial in maintaining political and economic power, but even the best navigators had difficulty in knowing where they were in the open sea. North-south position (latitude) could be worked out using well-established methods, but accurate methods of calculating east-west co-ordinates (longitude) remained to be discovered. Charles founded the Observatory to achieve this through astronomical methods.

Built on the site of Duke Humphrey's Tower, Flamsteed House is the original Observatory building. It was designed in 1675 by Sir Christopher Wren, with the advice of Dr Robert Hooke. Its romantic, quasi-Jacobean appearance perhaps echoes the spirit of its predecessor, and it is in marked contrast to the classical 'modernism' of the Queen's House below. The site was chosen because of its height and clear fields of view; because its distance from London ensured that observation would not be impeded by smoke from chimneys; and because rebuilding on the foundations of the tower would save on construction costs. Flamsteed rather regretted this particular economy: 'It were much to be wished our walls might have beene Meridionall but for saveing of Charges it was thought fit to build upon the old ones which are some 13½° false and wide of the true meridian'.

Designed, in the words of Wren, 'for the Observator's habitation . . . and a little for pompe', Flamsteed House had domestic accommodation on the ground

FLAMSTEED HOUSE
The original Royal Observatory building, constructed in 1675–6, partly of recycled materials, and paid for by the sale of decayed gunpowder. It cost £520 9s 1d.

FLAMSTEED'S STUDY
The astronomer's apartments have been refurnished to give some idea of their original use.

and basement floors, with the Star Room, now called the Octagon Room, above. This was large and grand enough both to accommodate long telescopes and welcome VIP visitors, such as members of the Royal Society who came to discuss the latest developments in astronomy. Here also were two clocks built for Flamsteed by Thomas Tompion and installed in 1676, each with a 13-foot (4m) pendulum for accurate time reckoning. They required winding only once a year. Such was their accuracy that they enabled Flamsteed to demonstrate that the Earth rotated at an even rate, providing him with the basis for accurately charting the stars.

But it was in the shed-like Observatory – the Quadrant House – in his garden to the south of the present Meridian Building that Flamsteed did his main work. Here he was able to mount his sextant on a wall that ran truly north-south, unlike those at Flamsteed House. It was here that the first Greenwich Meridian was defined. The official Meridian later moved eastwards on a number of occasions as the Astronomer Royal of the day set up more accurate instruments with which to observe the passage of the stars.

The need for continuous observations meant that extension of buildings rather than replacement was the rule. Edmund Halley, second Astronomer Royal, built a new quadrant house next to Flamsteed's, and his successor, James Bradley, in 1749 joined a third one onto that. In this way the present 'Meridian Building' extended eastward over a period of a century, a process culminating in 1857 with the construction of the octagonal Great Equatorial Building, under the regime of the seventh Astronomer Royal, Sir George Biddell Airy. Its original

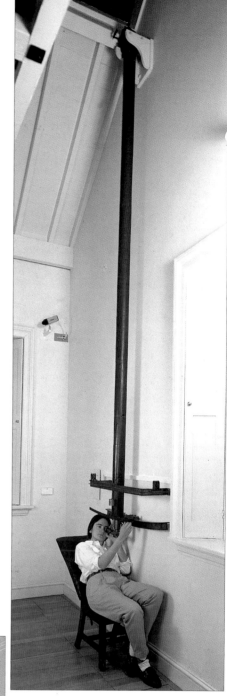

BRADLEY'S SECTOR
The Greenwich Meridian established by James Bradley, third Astronomer Royal, in 1749 is still the basis of Briain's land maps. This 12-foot (3.5-m) zenith sector was used at Greenwich from 1749 to 1873.

THE OCTAGON ROOM
Originally called 'the Star Room' when it was first engraved in 1676 by Francis Place, this was more for important visitors than day-to-day observing. The portraits set above Tompion's vital year-going clocks in the panelling are of Charles II and James II.

The Longitude Problem

Ancient and medieval seafaring was largely a matter of coastal pilotage and short passages from one recognizable coastline to another. With the long European voyages of discovery over trackless oceans, which began in the fifteenth century, a new navigation was demanded, based on observing the Sun and stars.

If seamen measured the angle between the horizon and the Sun as it reached its meridian, the highest point overhead at local noon, this could supply their latitude, their distance north or south of the equator. Longitude, or east-west position – the other co-ordinate needed for a deep-sea 'fix' – could not be found by such simple observation.

However, since the world turns through 360° in 24 hours, or 1° every 4 minutes, longitude was theoretically measurable in terms of time. The Sun told the navigator when it was noon on his own meridian. If he also knew the exact time, at the same moment, on another fixed or 'prime' meridian to east or west, his longitude would be the time difference between the two

JOHN FLAMSTEED
Born in 1646, Flamsteed was appointed first Astronomer Royal at Greenwich in 1675 and died in the post in 1719. His 44 years of charting the heavens was the foundation of all subsequent work at Greenwich. From a portrait by Thomas Gibson.

meridians expressed as the angle between them at the Earth's axis. As the Earth is some 24,900 miles around (40,090 km), each degree of longitude measured at its axis represents about 69 miles (111 km) along the equator, decreasing at a regular rate as the meridians – the lines of longitude – converge to meet at the poles.

All this was known when John Flamsteed became first Astronomer Royal at Greenwich in 1675. The problem was the impossibility of making a clock that would accurately keep the time of a prime meridian at sea, to compare with local 'sun time'. There were also no accurate celestial charts or tables to do the necessary calculations, or to work out time differences by astronomical means – which was also theoretically possible.

THE FIRST 'SEA-CLOCK'
John Harrison completed 'H1', his first large timekeeper (left), in 1735. He finished his perfected prototype 'H4' in 1759 (see p. 3).

Flamsteed and his successors applied themelves to the astronomical tasks, eventually with success. But it was the clockmaker John Harrison, by perfecting the marine timekeeper, or 'chronometer', in 1759, who put longitude calculation within reach of most seamen – at almost exactly the same time. Skilled navigators such as Captain Cook, who proved the reliability of Harrison's invention on his Pacific voyage of 1772–5, in fact did so by using the astronomical method for comparison. Moreover, the calculations needed for both relied on the tables of the *Nautical Almanac*, first published by the fifth Astronomer Royal at Greenwich, Nevil Maskelyne, in 1766 – and every year since.

NIGHT LINE
Longitude 0° at the Observatory, as defined by Airy's Transit Circle from 1851; Prime Meridian of the world since 1884.

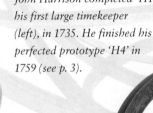

SEA ASTROLABE
An early instrument for measuring the angular height of stars or Sun over the horizon to determine latitude.

drum-shaped telescope dome, possibly made of papier-mâché, was replaced with a distinctive onion-shaped dome in 1892–3. The dome to house the new 28-inch refracting telescope was removed in 1953 after being wrecked by a near miss from a V1 flying bomb in 1944. It was replaced by a fibreglass replica in 1975. The pedestal of Wolfe's statue nearby still bears scars of the blast.

The Meridian Building provides a sober contrast to the picturesqueness of Flamsteed House, but under the eighth Astronomer Royal, William Christie, in a period of rapid expansion, there was a return to ornamental architecture with the building of the Altazimuth Pavilion and South Building – originally the 'New Physical Observatory'. Erected in 1894–9, to the designs of Christie and William Crisp, these look like two red-brick and terracotta jelly moulds. The small Altazimuth building originally held a telescope on an altazimuth mounting, enabling movement on both the north-south (altitude) and east-west (azimuth) axes. The portholes in the lower parts of the roof appear to acknowledge the continuing connection of astronomy with the Admiralty, which financed the Observatory at that time. The much larger 'South Observatory' was built in stages, a

WOLFE IN WINTER
The statue of Major-General James Wolfe, whose capture of Quebec in 1759 brought Canada into British hands, has overlooked Greenwich since it was presented by the Canadian people in 1930. Beyond are the Great Equatorial Building and Flamsteed House.

DOMES OF HEAVEN
The Altazimuth Pavilion, 1899, which now holds a photo-heliograph for observing sunspots, and the 28-inch Great Equatorial telescope dome. The wind-vane of Halley's Comet is copied from the Bayeux Tapestry.

COMPASS
An eighteenth-century sea-compass in the collection at Greenwich.

Time at Greenwich

The history of 'Greenwich time' goes back to 1676, when John Flamsteed installed his two regulator clocks by Thomas Tompion, 'the father of English clockmaking', to provide the accurate time-frame needed for charting the positions of the stars. One of these has recently returned to the Octagon Room. As the 'Greenwich meridian' that Flamsteed established was moved eastward to its final position, defined by Airy's transit circle of 1851, successive Astronomers Royal installed new and more accurate regulators (scientific clocks), which also made the Observatory the centre for testing the accuracy of new and improved timepieces.

'Greenwich time' was first publicly distributed by the Flamsteed House time-ball, installed in 1833 so that ships in the London docks could set their chronometers by it. Also in the 1830s, the wider distribution of Greenwich time was prompted by the need to co-ordinate timetables on Britain's expanding railways, and by the invention of the electric telegraph (1836). This brought the start of instant communications across the country; to France in

SIR GEORGE BIDDELL AIRY
Airy (1801–92) was seventh Astronomer Royal, from 1835 to 1881. From 1852 he transformed 'Greenwich time' from a nautical and scientific concept to a fully public one, by using the new electric telegraph to transmit it from the Observatory.

1851, to India by 1860 and America in 1866. By 1848 most British railway companies and the Post Office had adopted London or Greenwich time (23 seconds different), though the latter only legally became Britain's official time in 1880.

The Greenwich time service, domestic and foreign, which transmitted time signals by telegraph from the Observatory, was inaugurated by Sir George Airy in August 1852, using its newly installed Shepherd electric clock. This also regulated the time-ball and, outside the Observatory gate, the public clock, which to this day shows Greenwich time. The signal from Greenwich, operating through the nationalized Post Office telegraph system after 1870, regulated time-balls and public clocks at home and abroad.

In 1870, the American Professor Charles F. Dowd proposed that the Greenwich Meridian should be used as the basis of what became the world time-zone system. In 1884 the International Meridian Conference at Washington DC voted that Greenwich should be adopted as marking the Prime Meridian of world time and time zones. The French were the first regularly to broadcast radio time signals in 1910, and the 'six-pip' Greenwich time signal on the BBC was launched in 1924. Today, although the Prime Meridian remains that of Greenwich, world time itself is regulated by a dispersed system of atomic clocks co-ordinated through the Bureau International de l'Heure in Paris.

THE FACE OF TIME
The 24-hour Shepherd Gate Clock of 1852 at the Observatory, the first clock to show Greenwich time to the public, as it still does.

THE TIME-LADY
Ruth Belville, the 'Greenwich time-lady', who until the 1930s used a pocket chronometer checked at the Observatory gate to carry accurate time to London's chronometer makers.

SUN AND MOON FIGURE (below)
The South Building's elaborate terracotta decoration includes the names of famous astronomers and instrument makers, with a bust of John Flamsteed over the entrance.

THE SOUTH BUILDING
Originally the New Physical Observatory, completed in 1899, this was new accommodation for the scientific departments of the Royal Observatory, with a large telescope in the roof dome. It now holds the RO/NMM Modern Astronomy section and the Museum's Planetarium.

tribute to Christie's persistence in pressing for funding. Its telescope dome now houses the Observatory's planetarium while the Altazimuth building holds a Dallmeyer photo-heliograph, used for observing sunspots.

City pollution, the building of Greenwich Power Station in 1902–10, and the disturbing effects of electric railways on magnetic observations, forced the gradual relocation of the Observatory's work from the 1920s on. Staff were redeployed elsewhere during World War II and afterwards scientific work transferred to Herstmonceux Castle, Sussex, rather than returning to Greenwich. The Astronomer Royal left in 1948, although positional observations continued to be made at Greenwich until 1954. In 1990 the organization moved to Cambridge but the majority of observations were then made at the Northern Hemisphere Observatory on the Canary Island of La Palma. The

buildings at Greenwich became known as the Old Royal Observatory, and in 1953 they were made a part of the National Maritime Museum. The Octagon Room was opened to the public that year, and in July 1960 Queen Elizabeth II opened the restored Flamsteed House. The complex was fully reopened in 1967. Ironically, the 'Royal Greenwich Observatory' (as the scientific body was known at Herstmonceux and Cambridge) was finally closed in 1998 and, although certainly 'old', the Royal Observatory, Greenwich, has now resumed both this title and the RGO's educational role in modern astronomy, as part of the National Maritime Museum.

THE TIME-BALL
Installed on Flamsteed House in 1919, replacing the first one of 1833, it drops at 1 pm, and was originally for ships in the Thames to set their chronometers.

Cutty Sark

THIS BEAUTIFUL TEA-CLIPPER, the fastest ship of her time and the last survivor of her type, is preserved in a dry-dock as a tribute to the ships and men of the Merchant Navy in the days of sail, and as a testimony to London's distinguished maritime past. Open to the public since 1957, *Cutty Sark* contains displays on the ship's history as well as showing the accommodation of the master and crew. In the enormous hold there is a large and colourful exhibition of ships' figureheads – the Long John Silver Collection – mainly from nineteenth-century merchant vessels.

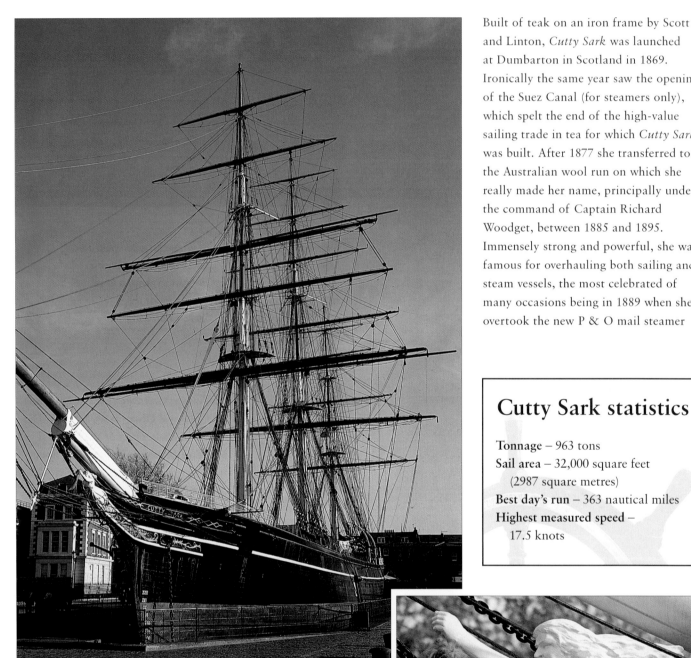

Built of teak on an iron frame by Scott and Linton, *Cutty Sark* was launched at Dumbarton in Scotland in 1869. Ironically the same year saw the opening of the Suez Canal (for steamers only), which spelt the end of the high-value sailing trade in tea for which *Cutty Sark* was built. After 1877 she transferred to the Australian wool run on which she really made her name, principally under the command of Captain Richard Woodget, between 1885 and 1895. Immensely strong and powerful, she was famous for overhauling both sailing and steam vessels, the most celebrated of many occasions being in 1889 when she overtook the new P & O mail steamer

Cutty Sark statistics

Tonnage – 963 tons
Sail area – 32,000 square feet
  (2987 square metres)
Best day's run – 363 nautical miles
Highest measured speed –
  17.5 knots

'WEEL DONE, CUTTY-SARK!'
The ship's figurehead is the witch Nannie from Burns's poem 'Tam O'Shanter', wearing the 'cutty sark' (short shift) of the story and grasping the tail of Tam's horse, torn out in her pursuit of him.

'WHERE THERE'S
A WILL IS A WAY'
*The stern
decoration of
Cutty Sark includes
this motto of John
'White-hat' Willis,
the flamboyant
merchant for whom
she was built,
around the large
letter 'W'.*

Britannia on the run into Sydney. On Woodget's first voyage in 1885, she first defeated her old tea-trade rival *Thermopylae* on the voyage from Sydney by a full week, arriving off the coast of Kent after 73 days at sea.

From 1895, *Cutty Sark* was in Portuguese hands as the *Ferreira*, but was bought back in 1922 by Captain Wilfred Dowman of Falmouth. In 1938 she came to Greenhithe on the lower Thames as a training ship for the Thames Nautical Training College. When no longer needed for this purpose, the Cutty Sark Preservation Society, formed in 1952, with HRH The Duke of Edinburgh as patron, ensured her survival. The ship was moored off Deptford as part of the Festival of Britain in 1951. In 1954 she was moved into her dry-dock, built at cost by Sir Robert McAlpine, and after three years of restoration was opened to the public by HM The Queen. The ship is now run by a reformed Cutty Sark Trust, which is planning further major restoration work to ensure her long-term survival.

Gipsy Moth IV

At the age of 65 in 1966–7, Francis Chichester made his epic, single-handed voyage around the world in *Gipsy Moth IV*, now preserved next to *Cutty Sark*. Designed and built for speed rather than comfort, *Gipsy Moth IV* covered the distance in 226 days at sea (with a stopover in Sydney). Chichester was later knighted by HM The Queen in the Grand Square of the Royal Naval College. If new proposals to restore *Gypsy Moth* to sea-going condition are successful, she may soon leave Greenwich.

GIPSY MOTH IV
The ketch-rigged yacht specially built by Camper and Nicholson for Chichester's single-handed round the world voyage.

MARITIME GREENWICH

'Greenwich affords one of the instances in which the monarch's property is actually the people's . . . for a nobleman makes a paradise only for himself, and fills it with his own pomp and pride; whereas the people are sooner or later the legitimate inheritors of whatever beauty kings and queens create.' Nathaniel Hawthorne, 1863

Top left: *the Old Royal Naval College with the Queen's House and National Maritime Museum buildings behind.* Centre: Cutty Sark *in front of the Pepys Building (now the Greenwich World Heritage Site visitor centre), with the former Dreadnought Hospital under conversion to a University library.* Right: *the covered Greenwich Market in the town centre.*

The National Maritime Museum

THE NATIONAL MARITIME MUSEUM at Greenwich is the largest of its type in the world. Its buildings include the Queen's House and the Royal Observatory, and its maritime collections are unequalled in terms of quality as well as size. They tell the story of Britain and the sea, navigation, and the measurement of time and space. Although primarily historical, the displays also cover modern issues such as global warming, the continuing importance of sea trade and the sea as a focus of leisure and cultural interest. Only a proportion of the 2 million items in the Museum can be shown at any time, and much is of research interest rather than for display. There are more than 4000 oil paintings, 70,000 prints and drawings, 2500 models, 3300 instruments, 50,000 sea charts, 100,000 books, 1 million photographs, 750,000 ship plans and 25,000 'antiquities' as well as 1.5 miles (3 km) of shelved manuscripts. It also has more than 100 boats, most of which are displayed at the National Maritime Museum Cornwall, which opened on the Falmouth waterfront in 2002.

While some of the collections go back centuries, the Museum was founded by Act of Parliament only in 1934, and opened in the Queen's House and adjoining buildings in 1937. The two inner wings were added to the House in 1807–11 to convert it into a vast school, the Royal Naval Asylum. This was established at Greenwich by Royal Warrant in 1805 to accommodate 700 boys and (until 1841) 300 girls, and was quite separate from the Greenwich Hospital School, which educated 'orphans of the sea' from 1715 on.

The architect of these extensions was Daniel Asher Alexander, after he suggested that 'the architect be directed to form his plan in strict accordance with the style of Inigo Jones'. He was immediately given the job and produced a very sympathetic result, including the fine colonnades that served as covered play areas for the children.

The Asylum was taken over by Greenwich Hospital in 1821. Combined with its own school as the Upper and Lower Schools of Greenwich Hospital, it was organizationally reformed and extended with a south and outer west wing in 1861–2, designed by Philip Charles Hardwick. In 1873 an iron-vaulted gymnasium known as 'Neptune's Hall' was added between the two west wings, behind the imposing Doric façade that now forms the Museum's North Entrance. A large dining hall and dormitory wing were the final additions on the west side in 1876, and the whole complex was renamed the Royal Hospital School in 1892.

THE MAIN ENTRANCE
This imposing façade dates from 1873, although the area behind, now Neptune Court, was totally redeveloped from 1996-99.

MAP OF THE NEW WORLD AFTER 1492
This map has meridians and parallels drawn for every 10° and is surrounded by twelve heads, representing the twelve winds. Coloured engraving by Francesco Rosselli, about 1508.

After the school moved out to Suffolk in 1933, the buildings were converted to house the new Museum, largely at the cost of Sir James Caird (1864–1954), a Scottish ship-owner who was the National Maritime Museum's greatest benefactor. He had already been the main private backer in preserving Nelson's flagship *Victory* at Portsmouth, and eventually put over £1.25 million into acquisitions and buildings for the Museum, working with its Trustees and first Director, Sir Geoffrey Callender: £100 million would hardly match this generosity today. During the conversion a top-lit rotunda by Sir Edwin Lutyens was inserted into Alexander's west wing, honouring Sir James. The Greenwich Hospital collection of paintings, displayed in the Painted Hall of the Royal Naval College, and material from the former Royal Naval Museum there were transferred to the new Museum's care in 1936. The Observatory buildings were added in the 1950s.

Neptune's Hall was used for the royal opening by King George VI in 1937, and afterwards it became a display area for

NEPTUNE COURT
The view over the Upper Court, looking south west, with the interactive 'Making Waves' display along East Street.

SHIP MODEL
Model of a 50-gun ship of about 1710, once owned by an admiral who fought in the American War of Independence.

boats, models and other large objects until 1972, when it was redesigned as the new 'Neptune Hall' with the 1907 paddle-tug *Reliant* as centrepiece. This lasted until 1997, when the entire Hall was dismantled in a £20-million Lottery-funded redevelopment by Rick Mather Associates and the Building Design Partnership. The façade remains but behind it a vast atrium, the 'Neptune Court', now forms the centre of the Museum beneath a glass and steel roof that spans the whole area between the 1807–62 west wings.

THE GALLERIES
The North Entrance leads from the direction of the town centre, Greenwich Pier and the Royal Naval College into Neptune Court, and visitors are able easily to circulate from there to all other public areas of the surrounding North, South, East, West and South-West Galleries. All levels are served by lifts as well as stairs.

'ENGLAND EXPECTS . . .'
J. M. W. Turner's painting of Victory *at the Battle of Trafalgar was commissioned by George IV. The only painting by Turner in the Royal Collection, it proved so controversial that the King gave it to Greenwich Hospital in 1829.*

ROYAL FASHION
This sailor suit made on board the Royal Yacht for King Edward VII, as 6-year-old Prince of Wales in 1846, started a fashion which still endures in civilian clothing.

The cube and sphere on the Upper Court hold thematic displays on the 'Future of the Sea', and the Court Gallery beside the coffee shop at the North Gallery end is used for small temporary exhibitions. An elevated walkway over South Street connects the Upper Court with the Park entrance and Level 2 of the South Galleries. This also gives a good view down onto the polished aluminium hull of *Miss Britain II*, the record-breaking British speedboat of 1933.

On ground level, in East Street a large wave tank is the main feature of 'Making Waves', an area

which explains 'how the oceans work'. The galleries under the Upper Court include an object-rich display on 'Maritime London' and another on naval uniform and maritime fashion. East Street also features the Tarbat Ness Lighthouse optic. West Street is the 'shipping corridor' – with a turning bronze frigate propeller, an engine from the paddle-tug *Reliant* of 1907, and modern ship and shipyard models outside the 'Cargoes' gallery on the ground floor of the West Galleries.

Overlooking the whole of Neptune Court from the south wall are the figurehead and the reconstructed stern of the last

PRINCE FREDERICK'S BARGE, 1732
Designed by the Rococo architect William Kent, with decoration by the royal carver James Richards. Handel's 'Water Music' was probably heard for the first time from this vessel.

74-gun, line-of-battle ship *Implacable*, which was originally the French *Duguay-Trouin* and fought against Nelson at the Battle of Trafalgar in 1805. Captured shortly afterwards and taken into the Royal Navy, she was scuttled with full naval honours in 1949 as beyond repair, only these carved decorations being saved. Beneath them in South Street is the magnificent royal barge designed by William Kent for Frederick, Prince of Wales, in 1732. After his death in 1751, it became the principal barge of British monarchs until its last official use on the Thames by Prince Albert, consort of Queen Victoria, in 1849. Queen Mary's shallop of 1689 – another Royal river barge is displayed nearby.

The ground floor of the South Galleries behind contains a display on

Explorers

Exploration is a major theme in the Museum. From Greenwich, Elizabeth I saw Martin Frobisher sail for the North-West Passage and Drake leave for the first English circumnavigation of the world in 1577. Although pictures and documents relating to such early explorers feature in the collections, there is far more on later voyages of discovery.

The Museum's holdings related to Captain James Cook (1728–79) and his three great Pacific voyages are very strong, including two of the most important portraits of him, and a unique series of paintings of his second voyage of 1772–75 by William Hodges, who was on it. Some of Cook's instruments are also here including the first sea-going chronometer 'K1', of 1769, which the Admiralty issued to him to test and use on his second and third voyages. Cook himself was briefly a captain in Greenwich Hospital before his last voyage.

The Museum also has many items from Captain Sir John Franklin's fatal Arctic voyage of 1845, in which he and his two ships vanished without trace while in search of the elusive North-West Passage. It was only in 1854 that relics of his expedition were found in northern Canada and another five years before it was confirmed that all 138 members had perished. The Franklin relics were displayed in Greenwich Hospital during the later nineteenth century before passing to the Museum.

Charts, instruments, documents and pictures record the work of other Royal Naval surveyors in completing the picture of the modern world – all, from the early eighteenth century on, taking the measure of the globe east and west from the Greenwich meridian of longitude fixed at the Observatory.

Modern voyages, in which adventurers have explored their own limits, also have their place. The most striking example is *Suhaili*, the yacht in which Robin Knox-Johnston made the first non-stop single-handed voyage around the world in 1968–9. Now one of the larger exhibits in Neptune Court, this comple-ments the *Cutty Sark* alongside Greenwich Pier.

COOK, FRANKLIN AND RALEIGH

Hodges' craggy portrait of Cook at the time of the second voyage, 1772–5, and a Staffordshire pottery figurine of Sir John Franklin, a Victorian hero of exploration. Sir Walter Raleigh was an important promoter of exploration and colonization, especially in America. The terracotta bust is by John Michael Rysbrack.

'Passengers', which examines the various reasons for and ways that people have travelled by sea – driven either by need or more recently for pleasure. Models shown here include the great Cunard liner *Mauretania* of 1907 and the largest, of the giant new cruise liner *Grand Princess*, specially built for the display by the ship's Italian builders, Fincantieri. The West Galleries connect with the lecture Theatre through 'The Submarine' school-groups area, which also looks at aspects of the underwater world.

On Level 2 of the South and West wings are the Wolfson Gallery of Trade and Empire and 'Art and the Sea'. The for-mer shows how Britain established herself as a world trading power, largely by her command of the sea. The latter uses the Museum's superb art collection to show how the sea has formed part of European visual culture from the seventeenth century onward, in prints and paintings, and in the distinctive modern media of photography and film. It also connects to the Upper Court by a walkway over West Street.

MAURETANIA
The liner of which this is a model held the Blue Riband for the fastest Atlantic crossing, 1907–29.

Nelson (1758–1805)

Nelson, Britain's great naval hero, has always been one of the subjects on display at Greenwich – both by popular demand and because, since the nineteenth century, first the Painted Hall of the Royal Naval College and now the Museum have held much of the most important material about him and the Navy of his time.

Nelson was born in 1758 and died in his greatest victory, the Battle of Trafalgar in 1805, three weeks after his 47th birthday. A younger son of a country parson, he went to sea aged 12 under his naval uncle and, after some early experience in a merchant ship and on an Arctic expedition, rose rapidly to become a captain at the uniquely early age of 21. He commanded a frigate in the West Indies during and after the American Revolutionary War but, after marrying in 1787, spent five years at home in Norfolk before being appointed to command a ship in the Mediterranean at the start of the French Wars in 1793.

He first came to public notice for his unorthodox daring at the Battle of Cape St Vincent in 1797. Here, as a commodore in the *Captain*, 74 guns, he captured two Spanish warships, one of 112 guns. For this he was knighted and promoted rear-admiral. In 1798 he

'I Will be a Hero'
John Francis Rigaud's portrait of Nelson shows him as a young captain in 1781. By the time he wore the admiral's undress uniform coat at Trafalgar in 1805, he had lost his right arm and was loaded with decorations. The fatal bullet hole is in the left shoulder.

became Baron Nelson of the Nile after his epic pursuit of Bonaparte's Egyptian expedition ended at the Battle of the Nile, where he destroyed the French Mediterranean squadron. He was wounded there, having already lost the sight of an eye (1794) and his right arm (1797).

His affair with Lady Hamilton began shortly afterwards at Naples and created even greater scandal when he returned to England with the Hamiltons and continued to live with them, abandoning his wife. In 1801 his victory over the Danes at the Battle of Copenhagen broke a dangerous anti-British Baltic alliance and won him a viscountcy. After two years blockading the French and Spanish as Commander-in-Chief in the Mediterranean, he chased their Combined Fleet to the West Indies and back before finally defeating it, and dying, off Cape Trafalgar near Cadiz, on 21 October 1805. His body was brought back to England in the *Victory* and, after lying in state in the Painted Hall at Greenwich, was borne up the river and buried in St Paul's Cathedral.

Ship's Bell
From the foremast of the Mauretania *(see p. 29). Others in the Museum include that of* Vanguard, *Nelson's flagship at the Battle of the Nile.*

The top floor (Level 3) on the south side holds 'Oceans of Discovery', a gallery on exploration of and under the sea from the eighteenth-century to the present. On the west side some of the finest examples of the Museum's sailing warship models from the seventeenth to the early nineteenth century are displayed

in the 'Ship of War'. This connects with 'All Hands' and the North Gallery 'Bridge', both of which are interactive display areas, particularly suited to family and school groups, with displays relating to various aspects of life and work at sea. The North Gallery itself overlooks the whole of Neptune Court.

THE RETURN OF
THE DUTCH EAST
INDIA FLEET
*Admiral Houtman's
fleet at Amsterdam
in May 1599 by
Andries van Eervelt.
The Museum has a
unique collection
of Dutch and
English marine art,
of which this is a
colourful example.*

The Museum holdings on Nelson and the Navy of his time are the best in existence, and a fine selection of them are shown in the display devoted to him on the top floor of the South-West Galleries, opened in 1995. They include famous portraits and personal items, including gifts exchanged with Lady Hamilton and the uniform coat he was wearing when fatally wounded at the Battle of Trafalgar. The battle is displayed both in a modern computer-generated reconstruction, and by J. M. W. Turner's huge and controversial painting of the action (1822–24).

On the ground floor here (Level 2) is a large gallery now used for temporary exhibitions: one on 'Tin-Tin's' adventures at sea is planned for 2004 and a major exhibition marking the bicentenery of the Battle of Trafalgar in 2005. The Museum restaurant connects with this gallery, with an exit to the Park.

Many people use the Museum as a source of information, and the E-Library, which is between the South Entrance and the Caird Library (Level 2 in the East Galleries wing) is now the first port of call for some visitors. Here, computer terminals and other finding aids allow enquirers to tap into the huge hidden information and collection resources of the Museum or to gain access to the Library to undertake further research. While the National Maritime Museum has at least 500,000 visitors a year, its audience is much wider, through educational work and research links, publications, the thousands of enquiries it answers each year and its use of information technology to widen access to its resources.

FIRST FOR VALOUR
The first Victoria Cross ever awarded, in 1854 during the Crimean War, to Charles David Lucas of HMS Hecla, for throwing a burning shell overboard. It exploded before hitting the water.

THE BRITISH WITHDRAWAL FROM DUNKIRK, JUNE 1940
A painting by Richard Eurich RA. The modern collection includes a fine group of works by the official artists who recorded the Second World War.

The Thames and the Town

THE *PENNY MAGAZINE* IN 1832, in its item 'Holiday Walks', recommended travelling to Greenwich by water: 'the domes and colonnades . . . will rise from the shore, and impress your mind with a magnificence of which the architecture of England presents few examples'. This was shortly before London's first suburban railway reached Greenwich in 1836–8. For centuries the River Thames was a principal thoroughfare, and even today the drama of the river approach remains

incomparable. The full extent of the historic heart of Greenwich can certainly be best appreciated from a boat in mid-stream or from Island Gardens on the north bank, the eye being led from the riverside blocks of the former Royal Naval Hospital, up to the central Queen's House and then to the Royal Observatory on the hill. The riverside walk terminates to the east with the Trafalgar Tavern and to the west with the masts of the *Cutty Sark*, standing between the river and the town.

The historic town of Greenwich now has the late-Georgian appearance given to it by Joseph Kay, Surveyor to Greenwich Hospital. He not only made many improvements at the Hospital itself but re-planned the town centre in the 1830s, with the intention of separating the Hospital from the town and providing a grand approach to its gates. Supported by the Hospital's Secretary, Edward Hawke Locker, Kay wished to improve the 'circuitous, narrow and unsightly' route from the metropolis, which was further blighted by an open-air market. In place of the originally medieval town, crowding up to the boundary of the Hospital, he created a formal layout of commercial streets surrounding a new covered market, built in 1829–31. Originally, this had three principal sections, for meat, fish and

vegetables. Above the colonnaded entrance from College Approach there is still a warning to those contemplating sharp trading practice: 'A False Balance is Abomination to the Lord but a Just Weight His Delight'.

Today, the fresh produce has gone, replaced by craft and antique stalls, under a glazed roof installed in 1908. The surviving parades of stuccoed terraces designed by Kay compare favourably with contemporary schemes in the West End of London. He was responsible also for the elegant Trafalgar Tavern, whose cast-iron balconies, canopied bow-windows and an upper-storey loggia give fine views over the Thames. It was built on Royal Hospital land in 1837, replacing the old George tavern. Kay was not above abusing his great influence in Greenwich at the time, for the new lease was not granted to the

leaseholder of the George's innkeeper but to Kay's brother John.

To the south of Kay's rebuilt town centre is Nicholas Hawksmoor's remarkable church of St Alfege, a replacement of 1711–14 for the medieval church whose roof collapsed in 1710. St Alfege was Archbishop of Canterbury, captured and then murdered on the site in 1012 by a Danish raider wielding an ox-bone. This was the first of the 'Fifty New Churches' in London ordered under Queen Anne. Twelve were built, six of them by Hawksmoor himself and one of them by John James, his colleague at the Royal Hospital. James was also responsible for recasing the surviving medieval tower of St Alfege in 1730. The church was damaged by World War II bombing in the 1940s and its interior sensitively restored by Sir Albert Richardson in 1953.

ST ALFEGE'S
By Hawksmoor, 1714, though the tower of the previous church is hidden inside the 1730 remodelling by John James. It marks the reputed spot where Vikings murdered Alfege, Archbishop of Canterbury, in 1012. The window (top) commemorates the Elizabethan composer Thomas Tallis.

A Seaman's Town

Greenwich was always a place of river workers, fishermen and seamen. From 1704, when the first 46 naval Pensioners entered the still largely incomplete Royal Hospital, it also came to be a Royal Naval town. By 1814 the maimed and broken of the sea-borne wars that gained India and Canada for Britain, which lost her the American colonies and which defended her from Revolutionary and Napoleonic France, had swelled the 'in-pensioners' to some 2700. Wives and families came to live near their men, and many Hospital 'out-pensioners' and other seamen also settled locally. John Sykes, who as Nelson's coxswain twice saved his life, died in his 80s as a fishmonger in St Alfege Passage, in 1841. Wives took in washing or worked as servants or in shops. Pensioners, distinctive by their uniform, disabilities, seamanly bearing and nautical speech, thronged the narrow lanes, took the air in the Park and for a small coin or tobacco regaled goggle-eyed holiday visitors with tales of great battles, exotic foreign lands, storm and shipwreck on distant oceans.

Greenwich was a place of inexpensive and often licentious pleasures, with its riotous twice-yearly fair (to 1857), its pot-houses and taverns. The carved balconies of The Salutation hung over the landing place – for many trippers came by water from London. The Ship was also on the Thames, off narrow Fisher Lane

behind the modern pier; the Red Lion in the Dock pub overlooked the old market area. Pictures, stories and song celebrate the Pensioners and show them carousing in such haunts, refighting old battles over foaming tankards and long clay pipes. For once 'safely moored in a Greenwich berth', their main enemy was boredom: the Hospital looked after them well, but it was run on strict naval lines and they had few occupations – not even a reading room until 1828.

Offenders against the Hospital rules were called 'canaries'. They were made to wear a yellow coat and perform menial tasks, until this humiliation was abolished by Nelson's old flag-captain Sir Thomas Hardy when he was

'FISHER'S ALLEY'
A watercolour by Clarkson Stanfield of the lane that ran towards the Hospital behind modern Greeenwich Pier. It was demolished around 1840.

'BATTLES BY SEA AND LAND'
A Greenwich and a Chelsea Pensioner swap yarns in a print of 1801.

Governor of the Hospital, 1834–9. In fact, many Pensioners were quite young disabled men, and some lived to great ages, often over 100. One man who had been servant to Admiral Byng when he was executed in 1757 was still telling the tale after 1800. The last survivor of the loss of the *Royal George* off Portsmouth in 1782 died in 1840, and John Rome, the signalman who hoisted 'England expects' for Nelson at Trafalgar, died here in 1860.

The Park and its Borders

GREENWICH PARK TODAY still has some of the strong formal lines of its seventeenth-century layout, but overall it is more a landscape park of the eighteenth century. It has been open to the public since about 1705, although not on a regular basis until the 1830s, when it became locally notorious for 'improper' holiday behaviour by visitors. Set around the Park are some of the best surviving examples in London of affluent private houses of the seventeenth to nineteenth centuries. Within it, as well as Roman and Anglo-Saxon remains, there are many monuments, buildings and sculptures of note. Among the trees, the great chestnuts, some dating from the 1660s layout, are especially fine.

It was partly because of the height of the hill that Greenwich Park became the home of the Royal Observatory. The view that it provided of the stars was matched only by that of the Hospital and a distant London, a scene long exploited by artists. The famous seventeenth-century views by Danckerts and Vorsterman were followed in 1809 by the greatest of English landscape and marine painters, J. M. W. Turner, and by many nineteenth-century painters who were often more interested in the robust pursuits for which the picturesque landscape provided an ideal setting. The marvellously varied views from the hill, in ever-changing light, take in the sweep of the river around the Isle of Dogs, the former hub of a commercial empire. Westwards the eye is led, on a clear day, towards the dome of Sir Christopher Wren's St Paul's Cathedral. East and north we can see the surviving river-based industry and the Richard Rogers Partnership's Millennium Dome. In front, the cluster of modern Docklands is dominated by Cesar Pelli's Canary Wharf tower, No. 1 Canada Square, completed in 1991.

In 1835, the year in which a manually-operated rising and falling roundabout was introduced to a public agog for new experiences, the young Charles Dickens recorded his impressions of Greenwich Fair. For over one hundred years this was one of London's great popular attractions at Easter and Whitsuntide: 'a periodical breaking out ... a sort of spring-rash: a three day's fever, which cools the blood for six months afterwards, and at the expiration of which, London is restored to its old habits of plodding industry'. The principal day-time amusement observed by Dickens, 'is to drag young ladies up the steep hill which leads to the observatory, and then drag them down again, at the very top of their speed, greatly to the derangement of their curls and bonnet-caps' (*Sketches by Boz*).

An earlier observer had noted rather more than derangement. In 1730, 'great numbers . . . diverted themselves . . . with

RANGER'S HOUSE
The main part was built around 1700 for Admiral Francis Hosier. The writer and statesman 4th Earl of Chesterfield who later lived here added the south gallery (right). From June 2002 the House becomes home to the superb Wernher Collection, particularly notable for its Renaissance objets d'art.

running down the Hill . . . one of them, a young woman, broke her Neck, another ran against one of the Trees with such Violence that she broke her Jaw-bone and a third broke her leg'. When night fell, the action moved to the adjacent fair in the town where itinerant theatres, travelling menageries, such objects of curiosity as dwarfs and giantesses, and a temporary ballroom vied for the attention of the enormous crowds; all, in the words of Dickens, 'is primitive, unreserved and unstudied'.

Such excess could not continue indefinitely. As the annual numbers of visitors rose each year, so did the resistance by the local inhabitants who, in 1825, began a long campaign for abolition of an event that encouraged licentiousness and offended Christian morality. With the coming to Greenwich of steam ferries in 1836, and trains in 1836–8, about 250,000 were able to visit the Park at Easter and Whitsuntide. The protesters achieved their object in 1857 when the *Greenwich Free Press* reported the demise of the Fair, 'that old market of vice and debauchery'. Greenwich has been a tamer place since but with its resumed tranquillity, its majesty and its historical associations, the Park still has few equals as one of 'the lungs of London'.

THE LODGE
The Park Keeper's cottage by the Blackheath Gate.

While the Royal Observatory is the dominant structure in the Park, there are a number of others of considerable interest and charm: the cast-iron, pagoda-like, octagonal bandstand of 1891 and the delightful tea-house of 1906–7. To the south, at the Blackheath Gate, is John Phipps's lodge of 1851–2, a remarkably early example of the Domestic Revival style; to the north, by the road gate to the town, is the stuccoed St Mary's Lodge of 1807–8, designed by John Nash as an Italianate version of a picturesque estate lodge. Across the road from this, on the site of the demolished St Mary's church is Samuel Nixon's granite statue of King William IV, the 'Sailor King', erected in King William Street in the City in 1844 and moved here in 1936. Among other notable monuments, the bronze statue of General Wolfe by Robert Tait McKenzie, unveiled in 1930 on top of the hill next to the Observatory, takes geographical pride of place. To the west, towards Croom's Hill, is Henry Moore's abstract 'Standing Figure, Knife Edge'. Cast in 1976 and placed here three years later, it is an excellent example of Moore's late style and a wonderfully appropriate complement to a landscape that has been moulded by centuries of human occupation.

Framing the Park, Maze Hill to the east and Croom's Hill to the west offer a rich variety of styles in historic houses. Begun in 1718, Vanbrugh Castle, on Maze Hill, was built by the architect and playwright Sir John Vanbrugh as his own residence. It is the sole survivor of a number of houses that he built here for members of his family. The three-storey design with two battlemented angle towers and a central round tower, is

THE ROYAL OBSERVATORY
A view in morning mist makes the Observatory look more like a mid-European fortress than the first purpose-built scientific research establishment in Britain that it was.

dramatically medievalizing, its fantastic quality recalling Duke Humphrey's Tower on the site of the Observatory. Other properties of note on the hill include numbers 32–40, a terrace of five houses built by Daniel Asher Alexander in 1808–12 as a children's hospital and subsequently divided. Its site had been Greenwich Hospital's first burial ground, of which the enclosing walls and an officers' mausoleum survive.

Croom's Hill, the ancient route to Greenwich from Blackheath, has one of the finest concentrations of seventeenth- and eighteenth-century houses in London. The largest are at the top of the hill on Chesterfield Walk: Macartney House and the Ranger's House. Parts of the former (the home of Wolfe's family) date from the late seventeenth century, with extensions of 1802 by Sir John Soane. The adjacent Ranger's House is an impressive classical mansion, built around 1700 for Admiral Hosier, best remembered for his death from fever in the West Indies. In 1815, after some eighteenth-century additions, it became the 'grace and favour' residence of the Ranger of Greenwich Park. It is now run

BANDSTAND
The prefabricated Victorian Coalbrookdale Company cast-iron bandstand, 1891, still used in summer.

'STANDING FIGURE, KNIFE EDGE'
Henry Moore's sculpture, installed in the Park in 1979, looking east to the 28-inch telescope dome of the Observatory.

EASTER DAY IN GREENWICH PARK
An 1804 engraving of the Easter Monday revels in the Park, with sailors, Greenwich Pensioners, and behaviour proper and improper.

'At Greenwich lies the scene, where
    many a lass
Has been green-gowned upon the tender
    grass . . .' (William Mountfort, 1691)

*A traditional and sometimes dangerous
pastime on the hills of Greenwich Park,
notorious for creating 'sweet disorder in the
dress' of pretty girls. From an engraving
published about 1770.*

Sheriff and later Lord Mayor of London,
who then lived in the house. The most
imposing building on Croom's Hill, the
Gothic Revival Roman Catholic Church
of Our Lady Star of the Sea, was built
of ragstone in 1851 to the designs of
William Wardell, later an important
architect in Australia.

On the northern boundary of the
Park, the houses on Park Vista include
the last upstanding remnant of the Tudor
Palace of Placentia, a conduit house of
about 1515 bearing the arms of Henry
VIII. This is now part of a group of
houses extended in the seventeenth and
nineteenth centuries: The Chantry, No 34
and St Alfege's Vicarage. Across the road,
the early eighteenth-century Manor
House is an attractive example of its
period, with an unusual weather-boarded
belvedere giving a view of the Park.

by English Heritage and holds the
spectacular Wernher Collection of fine
and decorative art, dating back to the
Renaissance.

Further down the hill are late
seventeenth- and early eighteenth-century
houses and terraces. The Manor House
(*c.* 1700) near the top is particularly fine,
and the seventeenth-century Grange has
a splendid gazebo overlooking the Park
wall. This was designed by Robert Hooke
in 1672 for Sir William Hooker, the

THE DOME

*The 'Greenwich Peninsula'
has become Europe's largest
area of inner city regenera-
tion. Its centrepiece is 'the
Dome' – designed by the
Richard Rogers Partnership.
Twelve 100m masts support
the tensioned glass-fibre
canopy which is 380m
across, making it Europe's
largest single-span covered
area. Having housed
Britain's controversial
'New Millennium
Experience' through the
year 2000, the Dome is
due to become a 20,000-
seat arena for sporting and
musical events, as part of
a future development of
the area.*

A Greenwich Chronology

871	Alfred the Great inherits Greenwich from his father Ethulwulf and gives it to his daughter Elstrudis on her marriage to Baldwin II, Count of Flanders
918	Baldwin dies. Elstrudis gives Greenwich, Lewisham and Woolwich to the Abbey of St Peter, Ghent, in his memory
1012	Alfege, Archbishop of Canterbury, kidnapped and later murdered at Greenwich by Viking raiders. Later Saxon kings regain possession of Greenwich
1081	William the Conqueror confirms Greenwich as a possession of the Abbey of St Peter
1337	Edward III takes possession of the abbey lands for safety's sake but establishes a house of minorite friars (1376)
1414–15	Henry V confiscates monastic lands, and creates the manor of Greenwich, which later passes to his brother Humphrey, Duke of Gloucester
1433	Humphrey encloses the Park and builds 'Greenwich tower' and Bellacourt, the manor of 'Pleasaunce', absorbing earlier religious buildings by the river (–1437)
1447	Humphrey dies under arrest at Bury St Edmunds, possibly murdered. Margaret of Anjou, wife of Henry VI reacquires Greenwich for Crown
1485	Henry VII accedes and rebuilds Bellacourt/ Pleasaunce as the Palace of Placentia
1491	Henry VIII born at Placentia
1509	Henry VIII succeeds his father and marries Catherine of Aragon in the Chapel of the Observant Friars at Placentia, which remains the principal royal palace until the rebuilding of Whitehall (1529–36)
1511	Greenwich Armoury started
c. 1512–13	Henry founds Woolwich and Deptford Dockyards
1515	Greenwich tower rebuilt as hunting lodge. Tournament yard and towers built on site of NMM
1516	Henry and Catherine of Aragon's daughter (Queen) Mary Tudor born at Placentia
1533	Henry and Anne Boleyn's daughter (Queen) Elizabeth born at Placentia
1540	Henry marries Anne of Cleves at Placentia. (Henry marries twice more and dies 1547)
1553	Henry and Jane Seymour's son, Edward VI, dies at Old Court, East Greenwich. His elder half-sisters succeed, Mary to 1558, then Elizabeth I. Both continue to use Placentia
1577	Elizabeth watches Drake's *Pelican (Golden Hind)* leave for first English circumnavigation and knights him at Deptford on return in 1581
1585	Elizabeth signs Mary Queen of Scots death warrant 'from Greenwich, in haste'
1613	James I settles manor of Greenwich on his queen, Anne of Denmark. Trinity Hospital almshouse built; remodelled 1812
1616	Inigo Jones begins Queen's House for Anne, bridging Woolwich to Deptford road. Work abandoned at her death in 1619
1629–38	Queen's House finished for Henrietta Maria, queen of Charles I
1637	*Sovereign of the Seas*, the first 100-gun ship, built at Woolwich, using same carvers who worked in the Queen's House. Final armour production at Greenwich
1642–9	Civil War. Queen's House an official Parliamentary residence during Interregnum and, with Placentia, stripped of treasures. Placentia becomes biscuit factory and later prisoner-of-war camp in First Dutch War, then falls into decay
1660	Charles II restored to the throne
1662–9	New palace begun by John Webb. Queen's House partly remodelled for Henrietta Maria in 1662 and Park redesigned by Le Nôtre
1672	Willem van de Veldes, father and son, come to England at invitation of Charles II and are given a studio in Queen's House. Start of marine painting in England
1675–6	Observatory founded and constructed on site of 'Greenwich Castle'
1688–9	'Glorious Revolution': William III and Mary II become joint monarchs. Earl of Dorset appointed Ranger of the Park, with Queen's House his official residence
1692–4	Mary revives her father James II's idea of building a Royal Naval hospital, using unfinished palace site. She dies in December 1694 and William backdates founding charter to 25 October
1696	Wren lays out Hospital site and construction begins
c. 1699	Earl of Romney, Ranger of the Park, diverts Woolwich to Deptford Road to modern position (Romney Road). Ranger's House begun
1704	First Pensioners enter unfinished Hospital
1708–25	Thornhill decorates Painted Hall
1710	Old St Alfege's church collapses
1711–14	St Alfege's rebuilt by Nicholas Hawksmoor, tower completed 1730 by John James
1714	George of Hanover arrives at Greenwich to become king as George I
1715	First Hospital charity boys educated at Weston's Academy
1718	Sir John Vanbrugh begins Vanbrugh Castle as his local home
1727	George II accedes: Queen Caroline occupies Queen's House
1731	The 'Five-Foot Walk' between the Hospital and river granted for public use.

1737	Hospital institutes Greenwich Market
1751	Greenwich Hospital finally completed
1757	Admiral Byng detained in the Hospital prior to court-martial and execution
1758	Greenwich Hospital School built on King William Walk and boys transfer from Weston's Academy
1764–8	Hospital Infirmary built by James 'Athenian' Stuart (now University library)
1766	First publication of *The Nautical Almanac* by 5th Astronomer Royal, Nevil Maskelyne
1779	Hospital Chapel interior gutted by fire, rebuilt by Stuart and Newton and reopened in 1789
1783	Hospital School enlarged on same site by Newton (building partly survives)
1795	Princess Caroline of Brunswick arrives at Greenwich to marry George, Prince of Wales (later George IV)
1806	Nelson's body lies in state in Painted Hall before his funeral. Royal Naval Asylum (school for boys and girls) moves to Queen's House
1807–11	Queen's House extended by colonnades and flanking wings for Asylum
1815	Chesterfield House (now Ranger's House) becomes official residence of Ranger of the Park
1821	Royal Naval Asylum and Greenwich Hospital School combine under Hospital administration, as 'Upper and Lower Schools of Greenwich Hospital' from 1825
1823	Founding of 'National Gallery of Naval Art' in the Painted Hall
1833	Time-ball installed at Observatory
1836–8	Opening of the London and Greenwich Railway, the world's first suburban line
1841	Education of girls discontinued at Hospital Schools
1851	7th Astronomer Royal (Sir) George Biddell Airy installs new Transit Circle at Observatory and establishes modern Longitude 0° meridian
1852	Airy institutes dissemination of 'Greenwich time' by electric telegraph
1861–2	Philip Charles Hardwick extends west wings of School complex
1865–6	*Great Eastern* loads first successful Atlantic cable at Greenwich cable works. GMT transmitted to the ship through it during laying, for exact longitude, and to America on completion
1869	Greenwich Hospital closes
1870	(Merchant) Seaman's Hospital Society takes over Hospital infirmary as Dreadnought Hospital
1873	Royal Naval College transferred from Portsmouth and School of Naval Architecture from Kensington to occupy Greenwich Hospital buildings. School gymnasium, 'Neptune's Hall' built, later NMM large exhibit gallery
1880	GMT becomes legal time of Great Britain
1884	Longitude 0° at Greenwich becomes Prime Meridian of the World and official basis of International Time Zone System
1892	School becomes 'Greenwich Royal Hospital School'
1894	28-inch Great Equatorial Telescope installed in enlarged dome of Observatory
1894–9	South Building of Observatory (New Physical Observatory) and Altazimuth Pavilion built
1919	New time-ball installed at the Observatory
1924	First broadcast of Greenwich time signal by BBC
1927	Admiralty agrees in principle to transfer of Greenwich collections to a national naval and merchant service museum, when established. 'National Maritime Museum Trust' created
1933	School moves to Holbrook, Suffolk. Greenwich buildings reserved for National Maritime Museum (founded 1934)
1937	NMM opened by King George VI but closed during World War II (1939–45)
1939	Painted Hall restoration completed: reopens as RNC officers' mess during World War II and thereafter
1945	Decision to move Observatory's remaining scientific functions out of Greenwich
1953–8	Observatory buildings progressively transferred to NMM
1954	*Cutty Sark* moved into dry-dock at Greenwich, restored, and opened to public in 1957
1960	Flamsteed House at the Observatory opened as part of NMM by HM Queen Elizabeth II
1967	Observatory conversion as part of NMM opened
1968	Remodelling of 'New Neptune Hall' and most of NMM galleries begins (–1979)
1986–90	Queen's House further restored
1990	'Royal Greenwich Observatory'(RGO) moves from Herstmonceux to Cambridge
1992–3	Major restoration of Observatory
1995	Government announces closure of Royal Naval College in 1997–8
1997	NMM Neptune Hall demolished for redevelopment. Millennium Dome construction begins. 'Maritime Greenwich' inscribed as a UNESCO World Heritage Site
1998	Royal Naval College passes into care of Greenwich Foundation, principally as a campus of University of Greenwich. RGO closed; some functions return to Greenwich
1999	NMM Neptune Court redevelopment completed. Docklands Light Railway opened to Greenwich.
2000	'New Millennium Experience' open all year in the Dome.
2001	University of Greenwich and Trinity College of Music complete restoration of and move into all the Old Royal Naval College buildings

Gazetteer

The entries are arranged in the following order:

Major buildings
Riverfront
Greenwich Park
Park Borders
Town Centre
Statues

All buildings marked * are either private or have no general public access.

Although most of the features listed lie within the World Heritage Site, the boundary of which is indicated by the dotted line on the map, others have been included for general information.

MAJOR BUILDINGS

See pp. 10–15.

❸ ❹ ❺ and ❻ are now University of Greenwich buildings; ❷ will be occupied by Trinity College of Music.

OLD ROYAL NAVAL COLLEGE
❶ **West Gate**
> Designed by Thomas Ripley, 1749–51. The celestial and terrestrial globes on the pillars commemorate Commodore Anson's circumnavigation of 1740–4 in the

West Gate of the Old Royal Naval College

Centurion, *his track originally being marked on the latter. The gate was closer to the buildings until it was moved in 1849–50, when Philip Hardwick also built the East Gate on Park Row.*

❷ **King Charles Court** *
> *The east range, the first wing of Charles II's proposed royal palace, was built by John Webb, 1664–9, and remodelled for the Royal Hospital by Sir Christopher Wren and Nicholas Hawksmoor, 1696–1707. The west range was built by John Yenn, 1812–15, replacing building of 1696–1704 by Wren, the north end*

The Trafalgar Quarters

pavilion by Hawksmoor, 1712–15, and the south end pavilion by James Stuart, 1769–74. Joshua Marshall's carvings in the east pediment show the Stuart royal arms supported by figures of Fortitude and Dominion of the Seas and, in the north, the same arms supported by Mars and Fame.

❸ **King William Court**
(* except Painted Hall)
> *Designed and begun by Wren and finished under the direction of Hawksmoor and Vanbrugh, 1698–1728. Sir James Thornhill decorated the Painted Hall ceiling 1708–25. The painting celebrates the triumph of Protestant peace, with William and Mary attended by the Virtues presenting the cap of Liberty to Europe above the crouching figure of tyranny, in the form of Louis XIV of France. The Upper Hall decoration, 1718–25, shows Mary's sister Queen Anne and her husband, Prince George of Denmark, in the ceiling, and the Royal family of George I presiding over Naval Victory, Peace and Plenty. In the colonnade pediment, visible from the Hall, an impressive Coade stone sculpture installed in 1812, designed by Benjamin West, commemorates the battles and death of Nelson. Hawksmoor's brilliantly idiosyncratic west dormitory range of 1701–28 exhibits dramatic manipulations of architectural scale, set off with carved nautical motifs on the courtyard front.*

❹ **Queen Anne Court** *
> *Built by Wren and Hawksmoor from 1699, this only achieved its final form in 1748 when Thomas Ripley completed the end pavilions. Hawksmoor's arcaded centrepiece of the east front of the base block,*

1699–1705, is the most striking feature. A temporary chapel that he built in 1707 between the ranges appears on some prints and was removed in 1751. The early seventeenth-century undercroft of the former palace survives under the western range of this block, and the Collingwood Room above remains the size and shape of the original large Hospital wards.

❺ Queen Mary Court
(* except Chapel)
The last of the four Courts, it was laid out by Wren but not built until 1735–51 by Ripley. Ripley's chapel interior burnt out in 1779 and its replacement is the late Greek-revival masterpiece of James Stuart assisted by William Newton, 1779–89. The altarpiece, 1789, showing St Paul surviving the bite of a viper, after shipwreck on Malta, is the only major painting by Sir Benjamin West PRA still in the location for which it was painted.

❻ Former Dreadnought Seamen's Hospital (*except restaurant)
This was originally the Greenwich Hospital Infirmary, built by James Stuart, 1764–8, with a freestanding ward added on the west side in 1808–10. It was partially rebuilt after a fire in 1811 and substantially

The Queen's House

modified by Joseph Kay in the 1830s and 1840s. The building was leased in 1870 to the (merchant) Seamen's Hospital Society to replace the hospital ship Dreadnought, *formerly moored off Greenwich. It is now the Dreadnought Library of the University*.*

❼ Pepys Building
Put up between 1874 and 1883, it was originally fives and racquets courts for the Royal Naval College, flanking an open central courtyard. The court was roofed over for a mechanical laboratory in about 1906. The building is mainly notable for its imposing river façade, inset with busts of British naval heroes. It is now the Greenwich Gateway World Heritage Site Visitor Centre. The former Hospital stable block between the Pepys Building and the West Gate was built by Joseph Kay in 1836, at that time outside the Hospital grounds.

❽ Devonport House* and the Hospital Burial Ground.
Built on the site of the burial ground by Sir Edwin Cooper, 1925–34, as a nurses home, this incorporates two-thirds of Newton's Greenwich Hospital School building of 1783–4 as a rear wing. It is now partly a student residence and partly a conference centre for the University of Greenwich. The cemetery was closed in

1857, but Ripley's mausoleum of 1750 and some graves around it remain. Captain Hardy of the Victory, *later an admiral and Governor of the Hospital, 1834–9, is buried in the vault and Nelson's servant Tom Allen nearby.*

❾ Trafalgar Quarters *
Built by John Yenn, 1813–16, these handsome brick and stone offices have the Hospital arms in Coade stone over the central bays, and matching lodges. It was here that out-pensions were administered and the Hospital's income calculated. It was later part of the Royal Hospital School and has now been converted into sheltered accommodation for the seafarers' dependents by Greenwich Hospital.

NATIONAL MARITIME MUSEUM.
See p. 48 for all NMM enquiries.

❿ NMM Galleries
See pp. 26–31.
Architects responsible for construction of the Museum were: Daniel Asher Alexander, 1807–11; Philip Charles Hardwick, 1861–2; Admiralty architects under Captain A. Clarke, 1872–3; Colonel Charles Pasley, 1876; A. J. Pitcher with Sir Edwin Lutyens, 1934–7; Rick Mather Associates and Building Design Partnership, 1997–9. Alexander added the Tuscan

John Adams, Greenwich Pensioner, 1840

The courtyard of the Observatory

colonnades and immediately flanking wings to the Queen's House from 1807 for the Royal Naval Asylum, subsequently the Royal Hospital School. Other additions including Neptune Hall, (the 1873 gymnasium behind the Doric north frontispiece) were made up to 1876. During the NMM conversion Lutyens inserted a top-lit vestibule commemorating the Museum's benefactor Sir James Caird into Alexander's west wing. 1990s work removed the Neptune Hall, replacing it with a high-level glass roof that forms a much larger covered courtyard between the Alexander and Hardwick ranges.

⓫ NMM Administration
(*business visitors only)
Alexander's east wing of 1807–11 was adapted to Museum use in 1950–1, after wartime occupation by the Admiralty. The eastern entrance from Park Vista was inserted in the 1930s.

⓬ The Queen's House
See pp. 6–9.
Built by Inigo Jones for Queen Anne of Denmark and Queen Henrietta Maria, 1616–35, with additions in 1662. One of the most important buildings in British architectural history, the building is now the centrepiece of the NMM and usually displays works from the Museum's superb art collection. Begun as an addition to the brick palace of Placentia, it was originally an H-block, with a central bridge spanning the old Deptford to Woolwich road. After the Restoration, the upper floor was altered to a fully connected square layout, with sets of apartments for the king and queen. The cubic galleried Hall, the dramatic Tulip Stairs, the mid-seventeenth-century plasterwork of the Bridge Rooms, and the loggia offering views of the Park and the Observatory, give a flavour of palatial splendour.

⓭ The Royal Observatory
See pp. 16–21.
Flamsteed House, the oldest part, was designed by Wren and Robert Hooke, 1675–6, and built on the foundations of the former Greenwich Castle/Duke Humphrey's Tower. Wren described it as 'for the observator's habitation and a little for pompe'. All the early Astronomers Royal lived as well as worked there, though the Octagon Room was more useful for 'pompe' than regular obser-
vation. John Flamsteed, the first Astronomer Royal (from 1675) immediately set up a more utilitarian sextant and quadrant house in the garden, part of which survives. His successor Edmond Halley built an adjoining one, extended west-ward by Board of Ordnance Engineers, 1749–1813, and Admiralty Engineers and

The Observatory as seen from the Queen's House loggia

Architects, 1851–95, to form the present Meridian Building and Great Equatorial Building. Longitude 0°, as defined by the seventh Astronomer Royal, Sir George Biddell Airy, passes through this building. The red-brick and terracotta Altazimuth Pavilion and South Building were designed by William Crisp, 1894–5, in a period of rapid expansion of scientific work. Beside the South Building is part of William Herschel's 40-foot (12 m) telescope tube. The time-ball on the east turret of Flamsteed House has indicated Greenwich Mean Time since 1833 by dropping at 1 pm precisely. The present ball dates from 1919.

⓭ Observatory Planetarium (in South Building)
48 seats only. Also Altazimuth Pavilion: demonstration and schools use only.

RIVERFRONT

⓮ Five-Foot Walk
Granted by Greenwich Hospital in 1731 as a public right of way between the buildings and the river,

the name comes from its original width. The river walk now extends east to the Millennium Dome and west to the new Greenwich Reach developments flanking Deptford Creek.

⓯ *Cutty Sark* and *Gipsy Moth IV*, Cutty Sark Gardens

See pp. 22–3.

Cutty Sark is probably the most famous and beautiful, and the last surviving, tea-clipper. She was also the fastest sailing ship of her time. Designed for the China tea run she was launched by Scott and Linton of Dumbarton in 1869, the year that the opening of the Suez Canal undermined this trade for sailing ships. Her fastest passages were made in the Australian wool trade, to which she turned after 1877. Later in Portuguese ownership, she survived to become a moored training vessel before being brought into permanent dry-dock here in 1954, commemorating London's maritime past and the merchant ships and crews of the days of sail. Cutty Sark Gardens, an entirely modern space, was formerly filled by the riverfront Ship Hotel and surrounding buildings, destroyed in World War II.

⓰ Greenwich Foot Tunnel

Built by Alexander Binnie, London County Council, 1900–2, originally so that workers from south of the river could reach the London Docks. It is well worth going through the tile-glazed tunnel for the classic 'Canaletto' view of Greenwich from Island Gardens on the other side (beside the next Docklands Light Railway station toward London). The modern lifts preserve the original mahogany-lined cabins.

⓱ Greenwich Pier

Originally constructed in 1836 for the growing steamer traffic, it is

still a major route for visitors to Greenwich by the frequent boat services. Plans to redevelop the pier promenade are under discussion at time of printing.

⓲ Trafalgar Tavern

An elegant building by Joseph Kay, 1837, which replaced the old George Tavern at the east end of Five-Foot Walk. Dickens, who knew it well, set the wedding breakfast in Our Mutual Friend *here: 'specimens of all the fishes that swim in the sea. Surely had swum their way to it'. Until 1883 it was noted for its 'political' whitebait dinners. After damage in World War II it was divided as housing, but was restored in late-Georgian style to tavern use in 1968. Crane Street behind it continues the river walk eastward and takes its name from the crane and wharf at which stone for building Greenwich Hospital was unloaded.*

⓳ Trinity Hospital* to Ballast Quay

On the river walk, Trinity Hospital is an almshouse

The Trafalgar Tavern

Trinity Hospital and Greenwich Power Station

founded in 1613 by Henry Howard, Earl of Northampton. The present 'Gothick' remodelling dates to 1812. Beyond the large Greenwich Power Station, 1902–10, Ballast Quay is an attractive river frontage of early nineteenth-century houses*, including The Cutty Sark pub. The view east to Blackwall Point and the Millennium Dome takes in Enderby Wharf, base from 1834 of that family's South Sea whaling fleet. Later a cable works, the first transatlantic cable, laid by the Great Eastern *in 1866, was made there.*

GREENWICH PARK

See pp. 34–7.

The best view over historic Greenwich, London and the Millennium Dome is from the Observatory ⓭ and the Wolfe statue ㊼ in the centre of the Park.

The lake in the Park

20 Anglo-Saxon Barrow Group
Thirty-one of these survive. They date to the sixth to eighth centuries AD. *Several were opened in 1714 by the Park Keeper, and others in 1784. Beads cloth, human hair and flints were among the finds.*

BUILDINGS
21 Bandstand
The elegant prefabricated structure, in cast iron, was built in 1891 by the Coalbrookdale Company Ltd. Summer music programme.

St Mary's Gate

22 Blackheath Gate Lodge*
Built by John Phipps, 1851–2, this is an early and robust example of the Domestic Revival style by an obscure official architect. It was built to house the Park Keeper as part of a campaign of improvements to extend public access.

23 Standard Reservoir
This was built in 1710–11 by master bricklayer Richard Billingshurst under Hawksmoor's supervision, in connection with construction of the Hospital. It marks the end of a long conduit that brought water to the site.

24 St Mary's Lodge
Built in 1807–8, this is an early example of John Nash's work in the Office of Woods and Forests before he became involved in Regent's Park. It is an Italianate version of the pic-turesque estate lodge, designed to be seen at the end of a long down-hill vista. Built as the Underkeeper's Lodge, it is now a Park café and information centre. This and the nearby St Mary's Gate take

their names from the church that stood by the latter until 1936.

GARDENS
24 Herb Garden *beside St Mary's Lodge*

25 The Wilderness *(deer reserve), flower gardens and wildfowl pond. No dogs allowed in this area.*

26 Castle Hill gardens. *No access to or from the Observatory.*

27 Ha-ha walk.

28 The Dell *and Ranger's House rose gardens.*

29 Dwarf Orchard * *originally attached to the Queen's House. A seventeenth- /eighteenth-century mulberry tree survives in what is at present a wildlife area only open by arrangement.*

30 Queen Elizabeth's Oak
This twelfth-century oak, dead for over 100 years and now fallen, was associated with Henry VIII and Elizabeth I.

For Park statues see p. 47.

PARK BORDERS
See pp. 34–7.

31 Blackheath
The assembly point of Wat Tyler's and Jack Cade's rebellions (1381 and 1450), and the massacre of Cornish rebels in 1497 (commemorative plaque by Park gate). Wide open spaces for kite-flying. Main line station in Blackheath village, 20 minutes walk from the Park.

32 Vanbrugh Castle*and Maze Hill
Vanbrugh Castle was built from 1718 by this architect, playwright and Wren's successor as Surveyor to Greenwich Hospital, who lived here to his death in 1726. Its medievalizing design is exceptional for its time and is still clear despite later additions. It is the only

Vanbrugh Castle

survivor of a group of houses he built here for members of his family. Nos 32–40 Maze Hill* were originally the infirmary of the Royal Naval Asylum, built by Daniel Alexander, 1807–12. They stand on the Hospital's first burial ground of 1707–47, the enclosing walls and the officers' mausoleum of which survive.

29 Park Vista

This connects Maze Hill railway station and the National Maritime Museum, east side, and has attractive eighteenth- and nineteenth-century houses*. By the Museum and Park gate the upper front wall of No. 35, The Chantry*, bears the arms of Henry VIII (replaced 1975). Although much of the building dates from 1800 and later, it incorporates sixteenth-century brickwork, the remains of outbuildings of the Tudor palace, see pp. 4–5. No. 34 and St Alfege's Vicarage are westward extensions of 1807–8 and 1829 by Daniel Alexander and Joseph Kay for officials of the Royal Naval Asylum and Greenwich Hospital. The Manor House, No. 13*, is an attractive early

eighteenth-century Georgian building with an unusual weatherboarded belvedere overlooking the Park.

33 Ranger's House, Chesterfield Walk

Built in c. 1700–20 for Captain (later Admiral) Francis Hosier, it has a handsome front elevation of seven bays faced in red brick, with a tripartite frontis-piece, a door-way with Ionic columns and a Venetian window above. Isaac Ware added the south wing for the statesman and author 4th Earl of Chesterfield, who lived here, 1749–73. The matching north wing was added between 1783 and 1794. It was official home of the Ranger of Greenwich Park from 1815, hence the name. The post was held from 1799 to 1812 by the estranged wife of George IV, Princess (later Queen) Caroline, who lived at Montagu House just to the south. This was demolished in 1815 but a plaque and a sunken outdoor bath inside the Park here mark the site. A plaque on Ranger's House commemorates the residence of Chesterfield and Field Marshal Viscount Wolseley. A superb building, it is now in the care of English Heritage. In June 2002 it reopened after major refurbishment and now holds the remarkable Wernher Collection of fine and decorative art, formally at Luton Hoo. This collection

is particularly notable for its Italian Renaissance material.

34 Macartney House*, Chesterfield Walk

Next to Ranger's House, this was the home of General Wolfe and his parents. It dates from the late seventeenth century, with eighteenth-century extensions others by Sir John Soane, 1802.

34 Croom's Hill

Winding up by the Park from Greenwich to Chesterfield Walk and Blackheath, this is one of London's best historic streets. Some houses* are seventeenth-century, some partly earlier, with later frontages. The 1672 Gazebo of The Grange, Ño. 52*, is a notable feature built for Sir William Hooker, who lived here from 1665 and was both Sheriff and Lord Mayor of London. Park Hall* just above it was built by John James, 1724, who intended to live there but never did so; it is also said to have been the local home of Sir James Thornhill. Heath Gate House, No. 66,* red brick of about 1630, is the oldest in Greenwich, completed even before the Queen's House. Our Lady Star of the Sea, the neo-Gothic Catholic church of 1851, is the first major work of William Wardell. It has a fine east tower surmounted by a tall spire. The chancel and chapel

The 'flea market'

Our Lady Star of the Sea, Croom's Hill

St Alfege's tower

of St Joseph were decorated by A. W. N. Pugin and the Lady Chapel by E. W. Pugin. The Manor House, below and opposite Macartney House, was built c. 1695–1700 for Commodore Sir Robert Robinson, a Lieutenant-Governor of the Hospital, and is one of the finest of its type and period in London. At the Greenwich end the Poet Laureate C. Day-Lewis lived at No. 6*.*

㉟ Fan Museum, 12 Croom's Hill

Occupying two houses in a fine and well-restored row of 1718–21, this is the world's only museum on the history of fans, exhibiting an important private collection. It includes displays, workshops, an orangery and a garden to the rear.

㊱ Gloucester Circus and Royal Hill

Leading off Croom's Hill, Gloucester Circus has a fine crescent of houses, 1791–1809, by the local architect Michael Searles. Royal Hill beyond has pleasant eighteenth- and nineteenth-century houses*, pubs and local shops. Further up, Hyde Vale and Point Hill both rise to Blackheath. There are good views to Ranger's House from the top of Hyde Vale and over London from The Point.*

㊲ Spread Eagle Yard

The Eagle was Greenwich's eighteenth-century coaching inn when the corner on which it stands on Nevada Street (formerly Silver Street) was on the main road east out of Greenwich. The archway into the vanished stable yard was built in c. 1780, when the name of the inn, now a restaurant and gallery, also 'spread'.

Spread Eagle Yard

TOWN CENTRE

㊳ St Alfege's Church

The architect of the parish church, the first of 'Fifty New Churches' ordered under Queen Anne, was Hawksmoor, 1711–14, with the tower by John James, 1730. The interior (restored after war damage) has memorials to General Wolfe, the Elizabethan composer Thomas Tallis, and the founder of the National Gallery J. J. Angerstein. All are buried here, Tallis in the former church which collapsed in 1710. Alfege, Archbishop of Canterbury, was murdered on the site in 1012 by Danish raiders camped at Greenwich.

㊴ St Alfege's Old Churchyard

Now a garden with a play area off St Alfege Passage.

㊵ Greenwich Market, Nelson Road and College Approach

This well-planned late Georgian redesign of the town centre was the main part of improvements carried out in 1829–49 by Greenwich Hospital, (which still owns most of it) by their Surveyor, Joseph Kay. Its formal, symmetrical stuccoed terraces were substantially complete by 1831, although the north side of College Approach (originally Clarence Street) is later. It compares favourably with contemporary schemes in central London. The glass market roof added in 1908 now makes it a lively all-weather space for craft stalls. The modern shops now facing in from east and west have also softened what were twentieth-century warehouse insertions for fruit and vegetable storage. Kay's fine pillared archway to College Approach still bears the sign 'A False Balance is Abomination to the Lord, but a Just Weight his Delight'. Above it, the Royal Clarence Music Hall operated for much of the nineteenth century. Attractive Turnpin Lane, at the south end of the Market, preserves a medieval street line, with a central arch through to the Nelson Road shopping parade.

Turnpin Lane

41 Greenwich Church Street

On the western side near St Alfege's, Nos 15 to 21 are a group of modest houses with shops of about 1700, Nos 19 and 21 originally being one building. Nos 15 and 17 are the taller and apparently earlier pair. Such late Stuart or early Georgian buildings are now very rare. Dr Johnson, compiler of the first English dictionary, lived in Church Street after he first came to London in 1736.

42 Meridian House and Borough Hall

This is a Modern Movement building by Clifford Culpin, 1938–9, on a Dutch model. Meridian House was Greenwich Town Hall to 1964. At 165 feet (50 m), the clock tower is higher than the courtyard of the Observatory.

43 Queen Elizabeth's College*

The buildings of this almshouse founded in 1574, by the historian William Lambarde, date from 1817.

44 Greenwich Railway Station

The London and Greenwich Railway was the world's first suburban line, 1836–8. It runs from London Bridge on a viaduct that may be the world's largest solid brick structure and, incidentally, gives a fine view of Thomas Archer's wonderful church of St Paul's Deptford which was, like St Alfege's, one of Queen Anne's 'Fifty New Churches'. The handsome station, built by George Smith in 1840, and rebuilt in 1878, originally had a high-level platform, lowered when the line was put in a cut-and-cover tunnel to run east beyond Greenwich in 1878. It is now also a Docklands Light Railway interchange.

STATUES

45 George II, reigned 1727–60; by John Michael Rysbrack, 1735. Carved at the expense of Admiral Sir John Jennings, Governor of the Hospital, from a block of marble captured from the French.

46 William IV, reigned 1830–7, 'the Sailor King'; granite, by Samuel Nixon, 1844. Moved here from King William St., London Bridge, in 1936.

47 Major-General James Wolfe 'of Quebec', 1727–59; bronze by Robert Tait McKenzie. Gift of the Canadian people, 1930.

48 Admiral Lord Nelson (1834), Dolphin Sundial (1977), Captain Cook (1996) in NMM south grounds. All bronze, the first by Sir Francis Chantrey RA. The leaping dolphins, by Edwin Russell and C. St J. H. Daniel, tell the time by the shadows cast by their tails. The Cook statue is by Anthony Stones.

49 Standing Figure, Knife Edge; bronze by Henry Moore RA, placed here in 1979.

Captain Cook

Information for Visitors
Greenwich Gateway: World Heritage Site Visitor Centre

This is beside Greenwich Pier in the **Pepys Building** (no. 7 on the map) in the grounds of the Old Royal Naval College, linked to the **Greenwich Tourist Information Centre** which is in the same building. The Gateway gives an overview of the history and attractions of Maritime Greenwich to help you plan your visit. It also has a café, a shop and a temporary exhibitions area. The Tourist Information Centre can supply information about transport, accommodation and events in the World Heritage Site, and about attractions elsewhere in Greenwich. For contact numbers etc., see below. Other up-to-date information on events, accommodation, hospitality, education and other facilities of Maritime Greenwich can be found on **www.greenwichwhs.org**.

GENERAL (See map for locations)
- **C** Children's Play Areas
- **i** Greenwich Tourist Information Centre
- **B** Banks
- **P** Parking. Car parking in Greenwich is limited and tightly controlled, weekends included.
- **PG** Police Station, Greenwich
- **PP** Park Police and Park Offices
- **PO** Post Office
- **WC** Public Toilets (including disabled except King William Walk)

Railway Stations:
- **DR** Docklands Light Railway; **MH** Maze Hill main line; **44** Greenwich main line and DLR
- **V** Viewpoint

RECREATION FACILITIES
- **31** **Donkey rides.** Most weekends and in week during school holidays (dependent on season/weather). Donkeys have been a Blackheath attraction for at least 150 years.
- **50** **Flea market.** Weekend antique and other stalls next to Greenwich Cinema.
- **50** **Greenwich Cinema.** Adjacent to town centre hotel; about to be enlarged.
- **51** **Greenwich Theatre.** Formerly a Victorian music hall, attached to the Rose and Crown pub here. Part of its 1885 façade survives on Nevada St.
- **52** **River Walk**, east to the Dome, west to Greenwich Reach and Deptford.
- **53** **Arches Leisure Centre.** Modern indoor swimming pools and sports facilities in a handsome building of 1928, in the style of a Roman bath house.
- **54** **Boating pond.** Usual season: April–September.
- **55** Tennis courts, cricket and **rugby pitches, putting green**.
- **56** Tennis courts and **club bowling green**.

REFRESHMENTS (Park area only)
- **57** **Regatta Café** at NMM
- **58** **Greenwich Park Café** and garden
- **24** **St Mary's Lodge Café.**

GENERAL ENQUIRIES
Greenwich Tourist Information Centre
2 Cutty Sark Gardens
Greenwich, London SE10 9LW
Telephone: 0870 608 2000
Fax: 020 8853 4607
E-mail: tic@greenwich.gov.uk
www.greenwich.gov.uk

For Greenwich Gateway and Old Royal Naval College enquiries, contact:
The Greenwich Foundation,
Old Royal Naval College
Greenwich, London SE10 9LW
Telephone: 020 8269 4747
Fax: 020 8269 4757
www.greenwichfoundation.org.uk

For all NMM enquiries (including *Cutty Sark* opening times) contact:
National Maritime Museum
Greenwich, London SE10 9NF
Telephone: 020 8858 4422
Recorded information: 020 8312 6565
Fax: 020 8312 6632
www.nmm.ac.uk

This guidebook is regularly updated but please note that museum displays mentioned in it, and other visitor information, are liable to change during its period of issue.

Picture Credits
© Crown Copyright, National Monuments Record: p12 (all), p13, p14 (bottom), p15 (top and bottom left), p40 (bottom)
© Bibliothèque de l'Institut de France – Paris: (ms. 1605): p5 (top)
© The Wellcome Library, London: p11 (top and bottom)
© Neil Gower: inside back cover – Map of World Heritage Site, Greenwich
All others © National Maritime Museum by Tina Chambers, Darren Leigh and James Stevenson